ROE STALKING
WITH THE EXPERTS

PETER CARR

Co-authored, compiled and arranged by
Peter Carr

Contributing authors
David Barrington Barnes, Mark Brackstone, Chris Dalton,
Dominic Griffith, John Johnson, Thomas Müller, Byron Pace,
Chris Parkin, Rudi van Kets, Andrew Venables

Design
Matt Smith

Editor
Colin Fallon

Cover photography
Andy Lee

Photography
Unless otherwise stated, photography is courtesy of the
authors

Printed in Europe by Cliffe Enterprise Print Partnership

Blaze Publishing Ltd
Lawrence House, Morrell Street, Leamington Spa,
Warwickshire CV32 5SZ
T: 01926 339808
F: 01926 470400
E: info@blazepublishing.co.uk
W: www.blazepublishing.co.uk

CONTENTS

FOREWORD

This book, *Roe Stalking with the Experts*, is a definitive collection of knowledge and anecdotes relating to the UK's native roe deer. It offers the stalker an in-depth insight into the deer's habits, and how to successfully and ethically stalk this wonderfully sporting species. Both bucks and does are covered; every stalking angle is looked at throughout the changing seasons to ensure you successfully put the right deer in the larder.

Compiled and co-authored by Peter Carr, the book also calls on some of the UK's foremost deer experts to provide their wisdom. These include such notables as Mark Brackstone, Chris Dalton, Dominic Griffith and David Barrington Barnes. Besides this collective font of roe stalking know-how, the book additionally contains some of the best roe heads recently shot in Britain with a complete listing of BASC trophy records, courtesy of the BASC and *Sporting Rifle* trophy measuring service.

Pete is known worldwide as an experienced deer stalker and big game hunter, mostly through his prolific writing. He is an award-winning editor of sporting publications, holding editor-in-chief roles on *Sporting Rifle* and *Modern Gamekeeping* magazines and a dual presenter/director role on the ever-popular 'The Shooting Show' broadcast on YouTube. He has hunted extensively in the UK, and harvested hefty numbers of all six deer species available to the British sportsman, as well as being fortunate enough to hunt big game across four continents.

I have known Peter for more than a decade, following his career progress and maintaining regular contact from his early days as a stalking guide and sporting agent. We initially met through a mutual army friend in Germany, when he organised a roebuck hunt to the Scottish Borders for a group of German and military hunters from the Osnabruck Jagd group, of which I was chairman. It was an enjoyable first experience and successful four days' stalking for all concerned. Peter's hospitality, organisational skills, knowledge of the species and attendance to duty were second to none.

This was the start of a long and dear friendship, and I feel privileged to have been able to stalk with a man of Peter's experience on several occasions in England, Scotland and Germany, gleaning from his vast knowledge of stalking.

On one occasion, after I retired from the services and took up the post of secretary of the north-east Branch of the British Deer Society, we were stuck for a lecturer (the scheduled speaker cancelled at the last minute). Pete dropped everything to come and fill the gap for the BDS branch, ever willing to share his wealth of expertise with a most interesting talk on big game hunting and roe stalking, brilliantly illustrated with some fantastic photographs, and amusing anecdotes, all of which was greatly appreciated by the members attending.

Pete is passionate about roe stalking, and although he has been lucky to have shot a myriad species including dangerous game abroad, the roebuck is still his favorite quarry. This is testament to his interest in this species above all others. He is therefore, in my opinion, the ideal person to compile and co-author this book.

The roe deer is held in high regard by many, and I would recommend this book to all stalkers who, like the author and his fellow contributors, hold a similar keenness for their pursuit. I'm sure it will become an invaluable reference source to all roe stalking enthusiasts.

Major Peter Beatty
RLC (Retired)

INTRODUCTION

There is no doubt in my mind that roe stalking is the *crème de la crème* of British rifle sport. I'm sure a number of colleagues north of the border would argue that stalking Scottish Highland red stags is the premier pursuit – and in fairness, I guess red deer could be considered more prestigious. Hill stalking certainly still has some Victorian airs of snobbery attached to it, and rightly too. We are, after all, a nation built on aristocratic traditions with a rich hunting heritage, and those prestigious airs and conventions are all part of that experience – long may it continue. But the lowland roe will be the 'bread and butter' for most UK stalkers.

It's no secret that roebuck are my favourite quarry, and my joy in their pursuit has not dimmed an iota in nearly three decades. Likewise, my five colleagues who have helped me write and compile this book hold the species in equally high regard. I have been incredibly fortunate to have worked with some of the best roe experts in the UK during my time as a gamekeeper, professional outfitter, and editor of *Sporting Rifle* magazine. The experts I have selected to feature in this book are all leaders in their field – not just on roe as a species, but on their role and pursuit in their own geographical area of the UK. If ever there was a dream team on roe stalking, these guys are it. I feel incredibly humbled to be counted among them.

These experts offer varied advice, backed up by experience, on what works for them – and by way of example, a selection of entertaining anecdotes has also been included. Much of what is portrayed is traditional management that really works. However, a more modern approach is touched on too: ideas and theories born in the field or imported from elsewhere. The use of trail cameras, feeders and deer plots to harvest deer may upset some of the old school but our burgeoning population of deer will need such practices to keep them in check, and crucially to identify specific animals. Through these pages the reader will have access to a combined knowledge exceeding 150 years collectively devoted to the pursuit and management of roe deer.

As I said, roe are the principal species for most UK rifle shooters, and after hundreds of years being classed as lesser game, the roe is now recognised as a sporting species. It may surprise some that this newfound respect is a relatively modern change in status. In Norman times the roebuck was classed as a beast of the warren, meaning lesser game as opposed to royal game such as fallow and red deer. This lesser status and subsequent persecution continued for hundreds of years, even until recent times. Edwardian sportsmen regularly shot roebuck and does on pheasant drives as the norm. Indeed, shooting roe with shotguns was still commonplace even in my youth. Thankfully better understanding and subsequent legislation eventually protected the species from being peppered – quite often with inadequate loads of inferior-sized shot.

What brought about this renaissance in roe stalking was the Second World War. Many returning British officers from post-war deployment in Germany had sampled some traditional stalking and enjoyed the respectful practices shown towards this prince of hoofed game. A few dedicated enthusiasts eventually secured the species the status it enjoys today, by respect, management and dedication. I wonder what those early pioneers, long in their graves, would think of the many thousands who pursue the sport in the UK today? It is their legacy we have in trust, and it is a responsibility we should enjoy, but not abuse, and pass on to the next generation of eager roe enthusiasts.

Taking on a deer-stalking lease is a serious responsibility with far-reaching consequences. Our main aim is to have a healthy, sustainable herd of an even sex ratio within the habitat – but trophy quality must not be overlooked. Deer management is a fickle thing, and all of us who have responsibility for deer ground play a very real part in the custody of the nation's deer herd in terms of quality and quantity. Our obligation is to manage them soundly, and according to best practice. If we do not, and shoot indiscriminately, I fear our enviable reputation for trophy quality will be lost, and the worst-case scenario would be for deer to be relegated to the ranks of vermin. The experience and advice offered by the experts in this book will help you get things right, maintain achievable trophy quality (every area has potential), and avoid the adverse effects suffered by mismanagement and subsequent damage caused by overpopulation.

Take Germany as an example. Broadly speaking, Germany's roe trophy quality suffered since the First World War, and rapidly increased after the Second World War. It wasn't just principalities that were shattered in the conflict – many great estates were broken up, and hunting concerns were fragmented into smaller and smaller areas. Unfortunately, today this has meant many stalking enthusiasts have shot promising young bucks too early, rather than risk losing them to their neighbours. Inferior beasts were often passed by in favour of promising bucks, and the subsequent trophy quality plummeted. This continues today – the few large estates that manage their deer correctly are surrounded by smaller hunting concerns that continually undo their good work.

Let's not let that happen in the UK. There is hardly a farm now that doesn't have someone who looks after the deer. We can work together. Shared information, combined with a joint management objective, is achievable if everyone concerned adheres to the plan. There is no reason why it shouldn't work – we are all sportsmen with a common aim and interest, after all.

Photo: Shutterstock

Population management of deer certainly isn't easy, and few amateur stalkers will achieve their goals every season, but a cull plan must be instigated and adhered to unless a dramatic change in circumstances requires a temporary cessation in stalking activity.

Holding too much ground, and by that I mean more than one can manage, is something I have seen often. Indeed I have been guilty of it myself in the past. Better to let someone else have a go and operate more efficiently on a more manageable piece of ground. Of course one can always enlist the help of those who are keen, safe and respectful of other forest users. Whatever we do, our collective management of the deer in our charge will be the benchmark that successive governments will use either against us or to support us. Let's ensure by example it is the latter.

Photo:
Shutterstock

Roe have to be the species most targeted by visiting trophy hunters. They greatly value the quality of British roe. Alongside Sweden we are quite rightly the envy of the world when it comes to exceptional roe heads. The recording of these trophies is of paramount importance. CIC had long been the body who solely held this responsibility, led by the redoubtable Richard Prior in the UK. Unfortunately CIC UK suffered some criticism a few years back under a new guard; much of it was warranted as standards had come into question and there was some associated controversy.

This led the British Association of Shooting and Conservation (BASC) to set up its own measuring system as a member's service under the safe hands of Dominic Griffith – arguably the best and most experienced measurer in the UK today, a former CIC measurer and trainer. Two years ago this service was re-launched in partnership with Sporting Rifle magazine and the result was staggering. The new service now records a very significant annual slice of all British roebuck trophies submitted for measurement. One of my greatest career achievements was to be part of this success, and indeed I actually designed the new medals. The last section of this book provides a full list of trophy records since the inception of the BASC/*Sporting Rifle* measuring service. It makes interesting reading and is an important record of UK roe quality. To say that it has been a runaway success would be an understatement – all credit is due to Alan McCormick, Dominic Griffith, Lewis Thornley, the accredited BASC measurers, and of course all those who have submitted their trophies.

I have been amazed at the response from you, the stalking public, who have embraced this initiative wholeheartedly with your support. Over the past two years I have been overwhelmed by the positive comments and encouragement you have given, and I can honestly say it is very moving at game fairs and other events to be shown someone's valued trophy and relive the experience to secure it in detail.

It certainly seems we have filled the gap admirably with our much-improved measuring system that crucially fits in with past records, making them still comparable. The slight method changes made are sensible ones, modernising an outdated system.

Meanwhile, after years of procrastination, CIC has decided after all to make no changes to the measurement of European deer species – but it has undertaken to ensure that age will have an influence on score by 2016. This will be interesting to say the least. We have always tried to allocate an age to the trophies we harvest and measure. Indeed we always try to encourage stalkers to target the oldest age groups. Nevertheless there is no ageing technique accurate enough to apply in practice and I can foresee huge arguments, and maybe even legal proceedings, where one stalker or measurer applies an age to a trophy that will affect its score and perhaps even its value.

I like to think I have enough experience with roe to age them with a degree of certainty, but I would never claim to be able to accurately age someone else's cleaned trophy, and all research in that respect has proven experts wrong. Quite frankly, this one seems daft. While seeking to remove the 'subjective' measurements, CIC is at the same time bringing in one of extreme subjectivity, or indeed even prejudice.

Thankfully the BASC system is based on sound science and practice. It is a service provided for British stalkers that maintains comparable records that will be a yardstick for future generations. Despite CIC's claim that our measurement bears no comparison to its own, the published records demonstrate that, as planned, BASC's are in fact aligned, benchmarked and consistent with theirs. Take for example Lee Mulcock's tremendous old Wiltshire head, which was measured as 187.3 by BASC and subsequently as 187.0 by CIC. There are now two trophy recording options for the British stalker to choose from. Both are set to stay, and the records of both are comparable with each other. Stalkers will continue to vote with their feet – of that I'm sure.

I hope you enjoy this book as much as I have writing and compiling it. There should be something in here for everybody with an interest in roe stalking. I wish you all fine mornings with a fair wind and accurate shooting.

Peter Carr
Yorkshire
April 2014

Photo: Shutterstock

WHAT'S THE BEST DEER STALKING CALIBRE?

D ebates will rage until the end of time about the 'best' deer-shooting calibre. The truth is, there is no universal winner – it all depends on what you plan to use the rifle for.

If you forced someone to pick their 'one-rifle' calibre for UK game, they would be most likely to say the .243 Winchester. It's legal for all UK deer species and a good choice for foxes too. For the larger deer such as red and sika stags, though, most would recommend something larger – a .270 if not a .308.

On the other hand, if you're after the occasional trip about, you'll want a calibre to tackle all UK species and the occasional safari or boar/moose hunt. In that case it's sensible to go larger again – a 6.5x55 Swedish or .30-06 Springfield.

Along those lines, some may complain that the .300 Winchester Magnum is omitted from the following pages. After all, it is permissible for all UK, European and US game, plus a good choice for all African antelope. For the regular travelling hunter, this calibre would be the perfect one-rifle choice. But it could be considered on the large side for some UK deer species, and Brit hunters may well want something that corresponds more closely to their 'bread and butter' stalking. On top of that, one may encounter difficulties obtaining a variation for .300 Win for UK deer, though there are a number of firearms certificate (FAC) holders who do possess a rifle in this calibre for deer.

What follows below is a short history and assessment of four of the calibres most commonly used to shoot deer in the UK. It is obviously not an exhaustive list, but for most UK hunters, it is certainly a good start.

.243 WIN

Like a large proportion of UK hunters, my first fullbore rifle was in .243 Win: a second-hand Sako 75 (a joint firearm held between my dad and I). This was to be our primary rifle for several years, before moving on to the 7x57 some years later. The calibre was of limited consideration – I knew little about it and was more concerned about getting a half-decent rifle. I somewhat shunned the default choice of .308 Win and .243 Win, chosen by many to tackle the UK deer spectrum. I saw it as following the herd. Obviously rifle availability was a big part of this, and it was self-fulfilling, as more people made a calibre decision based on off-the-shelf rifle opportunity.

I would say things have changed a bit now, and hunters have become more savvy. Custom rifles have never been so popular, and with that comes a calibre choice as long as time. Having said this, after shooting many rifles and calibres, I have come full circle and returned to the stalwarts of modern UK hunting. My last rifle purchase was a .243 Win Kimber Montana.

The .243 Win takes it parent case from the .308 Win. An efficient, short-action design, the .243 Win was a breakthrough in terms of factory-loaded ammunition. It allowed hunters to shoot one calibre for a large spectrum of quarry, with moderate recoil and excellent down-range trajectory. The 6mm bullet proved accurate and, as we have seen in the likes of the 6mm BR, this was just the beginning of its potential.

Loaded as low as 55 grains, and factory loaded to 105, it makes an excellent foxing calibre while offering good knockdown power for small and medium-sized deer. For hand loaders, tapping into the long-range potential of the 115-grain bullet is available but rarely investigated. Loaded with the lightning-fast, 55-grain varmint bullet, it easily surpasses the performance from a .220 Swift.

I have found the 87-grain bullet an excellent compromise to cover foxes and smaller deer species. Running out at around 3,200fps, you are looking at a 300-yard drop of six inches with under an inch high zero at 100 yards. This excludes one from hunting the bigger UK deer species, in which case you will have to step up to 100 grains. The 105-grain Geco is excellent for this, being a relatively inexpensive choice while still providing good accuracy with suitable carcase performance.

The 95-grain Superformance from Hornady is ballistically fantastic, but sadly can't be used at home on red deer as a result of legislation on bullet weight. In terms of long-range accuracy, many hunters will be pleasantly surprised by how good the .243 Win is, and my rifle is the most accurate I have ever owned, dropping bullets into less than 2in at 400 yards.

Interestingly, the .243 Win was intended as a long-range varmint cartridge, with barrel twists reflecting this. Soon people realised that the calibre could be used for much more than this, leading to where we are today.

It is tempting to say the .243 Win could be the answer to all, but be cautious. Beyond lightweight foxing loads, bullet selection for quarry type is important. At the top end of the .243 Win capabilities, it is a little underpowered, and placement has to be good. That is why some estates insist on calibres larger than .243 Win when stag season comes around. It does offer tremendous scope, if used with some thought and attention.

A Kimber rifle in .243

.270 WIN

I have to admit from the off: I have never been a big fan of the .270 Win. I always saw it as a lot of fuss and bluster for what it offered down-range. My first experience of the calibre was in the infancy of my fullbore rifle career, shooting a number of rifles on one cold range day. Among these were some of the original Mannlichers that were made so famous by historic African expeditions, along with an old .375 H&H, a well-used .222 Rem BSA, and a Parker Hale .270 Win. I came away from that day with no affection towards the .270 Win. There are some calibres, such as the 7x57 and the 6.5x55, that are immediately endearing. You feel like you want to shoot them more, just to feel the explosive combination of gunpowder, brass and lead again. The .270 Win just did not do that for me. I couldn't see why it was so popular.

Today, it still isn't a calibre I would readily add to the gun collection – but I have certainly learned a lot since that first experience. Turn the clock back as far as 1925, when Winchester launched the 130-grain .270 Win to the hunting public, and we see the beginning of a story that is anything but the success the calibre became. Instead of taking the industry by storm as expected, the calibre soon went quiet, more than likely owing to the popularity and availability of sporterised .30-06 Springfield rifles on the market.

Then, from the ashes, in a way I doubt any gun writer has ever done since, the famous Jack O'Connor rescued the calibre. It has always been unclear to me whether O'Connor was actually working with Winchester, but either way I am sure the company did what they could to encourage his promotion of the .270 Win. It is hard to deny that its early rise in popularity can be almost solely attributed to one man.

O'Connor went on to take a large spectrum of game from around the world with the .270 Win, although his wife, who was also an avid hunter, used a 7x57. During those years more and more hunters chose the calibre as a good all-round solution to North American game.

But as time wore on, we began to see cracks in the .270 Win. Most of these came in the form of excessive meat and skin damage owing to the high-velocity nature of the calibre. Some hunters began to note that although O'Connor had successfully used the calibre on big American game, it was far more suited to open range country on lighter game. Indeed the 130-grain bullet was woefully inadequate in the cold light of day when it came to efficiently hunting bigger species. Velocity

Common calibres: Which is best?

was only going to count for so much. There is a certain point when you need bullet weight to penetrate and kill.

You cannot deny that the .270 Win has proved incredibly successful, and to this very day, even in the UK we see .270 Win chambered rifles leaving gun shops on a regular basis. The Forestry Commission, certainly for a time, used it as its calibre of choice, and it was the 'go-to' calibre of the hill stalker for many years. That said, I doubt it would have been elevated to such heights without the help of Jack O'Connor. Certainly if we compare it to other calibres available today, I would suggest that the day of the .270 Win has probably passed; even a 150-grain .308 Win offers superior down-range energy. I have hunted with the calibre, fairly extensively in Africa, and I would take a slower, heavier calibre over it every time. That said, each to their own.

.308 WIN

As most people are aware, the .308 Win we use for sporting purposes leads a Jekyll and Hyde existence. On one hand we put lead down-range in pursuit of game, and target shooters make use of the excellent accuracy to punch paper at some impressive ranges. On the other, the 7.62 NATO arms our allies and our enemies the world over. There has certainly been a lot of bloodshed using the .308 Win in military theatres.

The history of the calibre is complex. It began life as a research request from the American government to the Frankfort Arsenal. They wanted to achieve similar power and range capabilities to their already established .30-06 Springfield, but in a smaller, more compact case. Reportedly some 10,000 prototypes were made before settling on the 'T65', which itself went through modifications over a number years before the final case design was agreed in 1949. Further testing continued until 1954 before the cartridge was standardised as the 7.62x51 NATO.

Pressure from the commercial world, and speculated leaks in case design, saw the chief of ordinance give Winchester the permission to use the cartridge in its rifles, and hence the .308 Win was born. But Winchester was not riding solely on the back of research completed for the government-funded contract. Indeed, in the preceding years they had begun their own development, testing the .30-80 WCF in the early 1950s. Standing these cartridges together, it would be hard to see the difference, and by all accounts it was a successful project chambered initially in Winchester's Model 80 rifles. However, from the limited information available, the calibre ceased to be a concern about the same time as Winchester was given permission to brand the .308 Win. It seems that having taken it to the concluding phases, it was easier, and one assumes more cost-effective, to run with a design that had been through years of development and testing, with the backing of the American government. The plus side was that the availability of ammo and rifles in

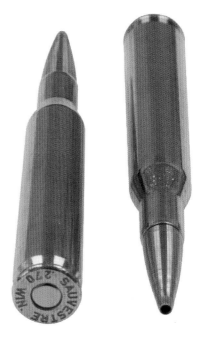

The .270 Win cartridge

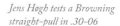

Jens Høgh tests a Browning straight-pull in .30-06

the future, owing to its military application, would help propel the cartridge to heights they could only have dreamt of otherwise.

The hunting world owes a lot to the development of this cartridge, which was one of the first that really went for compact efficiency. Previously, the focus tended to be on packing more powder in bigger cases, and little time had been spent trying to achieve similar performance from a smaller cartridge. The .308 Win led the way with this ethos, and more than 50 years on, we see the same push in modern calibre designs.

Byron Pace with a .243

Personally I have always shied away from the .308 Win. I saw it as the default no-imagination choice of so many hunters, although I would take nothing away from its capabilities. Time has morphed my view, however, partly as a result of testing so many .308 Win rifles for Sporting Rifle. The ease of use, ammo availability, undeniable accuracy, and sheer choice with regard to rifles and reloading makes the .308 Win hard to ignore, especially when considering the scope of game that can be taken with it. Certainly in the UK, there is nothing it cannot handle, and for the most part, loaded with the correct bullet weight and type, the calibre will tackle most game around the world.

.30-06

More 7.62mm – or .308 – bullets have been fired than probably any other calibre. Not only is it used currently by the US military in the 7.62x51mm NATO round, it was also used in the .30-06 Springfield service rifles adopted in 1906 for many combat roles, including long-range sniping. During World War Two America also supplied arms and ammo in .30-06 to many Allied countries, including Great Britain.

As far as sporting calibres go, the .308 is one of the most popular of all, leading to a vast array of bullet weights and designs. The .30-06, however, has been left behind in the modern world of calibre choice. Seen as dated and less effective compared to modern Magnums, this hugely successful calibre deserves serious consideration from hunters in every country, including the UK. Indeed, the usefulness of the calibre is reflected in the fact that every major manufacturer offers rifles chambered in .30-06.

The extensive history and reloading options for the .30-06 make this an exciting calibre to tinker with. Seen by Frank C. Barnes as "undoubtedly the most flexible, useful, all-round big game cartridge available to the American hunter", its hunting credentials extend back to its introduction via a bolt action rifle, the Remington model 30, in 1921.

Seen for decades as the standard by which all other big game cartridges should be judged, it's perhaps surprising to find that it performs very well even when pitted against more modern rounds.

For all antelope, deer, goats, sheep, black and brown bear, the 180-grain guise of the .30-06 is judged by experienced hunters to be able to cope with virtually any hunting conditions. In the past it was used for dangerous game in Africa, including lion, buffalo, and leopard, on a regular basis (although a 220-grain bullet was more widely used for the biggest and most dangerous game). Despite this, many countries ban its use on big game today – probably a sensible move for all but the most experienced hunter.

A 175-yard zero proves the most useful for the 180-grain bullet, equating to a 1.4in-high zero at 100 yards. Coincidentally, this is also the zenith (highest point) of the trajectory above line-of-sight (using Federal ammo with a Nosler partition bullet). According to Federal, this drops a 200-yard shot 1.2in below the aim point, with all shots out to that range within a 2.6in kill zone. This is very respectable.

Available trajectory data also shows virtual mirroring of the 150-grain .30-06 and .308 Win out to 200 yards, with the 06 falling less rapidly beyond the zero range, gaining 1.6in on the .308 at the 400-yard mark. On top of that, a super-fast (3,400fps) 110-grain bullet compares well to similar bullet loads from other calibres. Running it alongside the .270 Win shows that the .30-06 only starts to noticeably drop off from the .270 after about 300 yards – this despite the .270 packing an extra 100fps muzzle velocity.

So what use is the .30-06 to the modern-day UK hunter? Well, albeit at a stretch, it covers all bases. It is a little heavy for foxing, and can't boast the laser straight trajectory of a .220 Swift, but on other hand you can't hunt a bear with a 50-grain bullet, not if you want to stay alive. The 110-grain bullet will adequately take care of any deer in the UK, while heavier options give you scope for varying conditions, foreign travel and wild boar.

It doesn't do anything the .308 Win can't do cheaper, and in some cases more accurately. For hunting, however, this is largely irrelevant. So if you don't want to follow the crowd, and don't mind paying a little extra for the ammo, then embrace an old favourite with a long shooting heritage, and choose the .30-06. *Byron Pace*

The .30-06 can cover all bases for the UK hunter

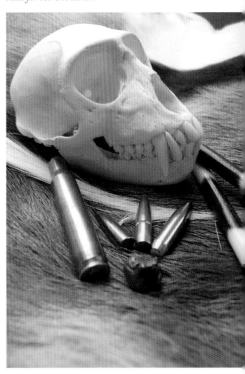

OPTICAL OPTIONS

One of the most commonly asked questions I hear is, "what is the best scope?" Well, I can tell you there is no magic solution to cover all requirements, so the first questions you must ask yourself are:

- What are my needs
- What is my budget
- What is my target species
- What are my likely ranges
- What light conditions will I be shooting in?

Concentrating on hunting optics, the species you intend to pursue is the starting point. Deer on open hills in daylight are very different to those in woodland at dawn and dusk; a 300-yard daytime crow is a different proposition to a fox at last light 50 yards away emerging from shadows. Many consider light gathering a priority, but light transmission is often the real consideration. A high-quality optic with a 40mm objective lens can offer a brighter image than a cheaper 56mm scope with all other variables equal, as the internal optics allow 90 per cent of the visible light spectrum to pass through with crystal clarity rather than leave you with a grainy, drab exposure. Objective lens size will influence exit pupil size, though.

When I started shooting, many European optics came with bold no.4 reticles, which, although fantastic in low light when engaging a fox and perfectly adequate in daylight on large quarry like deer, were of little use when varminting in daylight as the reticle obscured the target. With a reticle's centre subtending (covering) an inch at 100 yards and set in the first focal plane, when zoomed in to 16x and engaging a visibly larger crow at 400 yards, you were 'peeking around' a crosshair subtending 4in. Over the last few years I have noticed an increasing trend towards finer reticles, like the Zeiss no.60, which has fine lines from the perimeter meeting a discreet central dot. This style has appeared across many budgets, and offers an ideal solution to all light conditions when it is coupled with illumination. On the original, the dot is fine enough in daylight that any small target can be engaged at longer ranges, yet in lower light conditions or with heavy cover in woodland, the adjustable pinpoint illumination can be used to highlight its position for immediate target/reticle alignment. Cheaper illuminated reticles often flare out and destroy what image you have by being too garish and dazzling. The No.60 permanently changed my opinion of illumination for the better, and I have since seen similar sublime quality from Swarovski, Kahles and Meopta.

The argument of first (where reticle size remains in proportion with the image, 'growing' as you zoom) versus second focal plane (where the size remains constant to the viewer but not in proportion to the target) is fairly moot. Both have advantages and disadvantages relevant to your requirements, and the hunting world can accept either. It is what suits your needs that is important. With first focal plane you can aim off using the reticle, and it makes sense to have one with markings that match your turret click values. Second focal plane certainly makes more sense with hunting rifles where a slight 'aim off' within the kill zone is appropriate as it is the target you're using as a measure, not the reticle. For example, on a longer-range deer, you might prefer to aim a little higher toward the spine rather than start dialling corrections. Turret options like the Swarovski BT and Zeiss ASV+ have really made 'dialling' more fashionable to the hunter and are very effective in the right circumstances – but make no mistake, there is a lot more to shooting at longer ranges than turning a dial, both morally and technically.

What really differentiates European from Asian glass is the ability to resolve and aim at small targets at low magnification. I recently zeroed two similarly specified scopes at 100 metres alongside each other and at 12x magnification. The Euro glass was happily quartering a 1in orange patch whereas the USA/ Chinese optic at the same size of reticle needed a 2in patch to clearly hold centre. That is not to say either scope will not adequately assist your hunting activities, but the resolution difference is unmistakable. (But for treble the cost!) Where

A scope with zero-stop turrets

The Zeiss 60 and Vortex Viper reticles

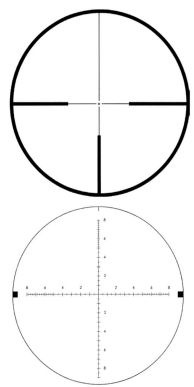

Simple, finger-adjustable clicks are desirable

WHERE TO LOOK

Zeiss
www.zeiss.com/sportsoptics
01223 401525
Swarovski
www.swarovskioptik.com
01737 856812
Schmidt & Bender
www.schmidt-bender.de
Leupold, Burris, Steiner
www.gmk.co.uk
01489 587500
Vortex
www.riflecraft.co.uk
01379 853745
Nikko Stirling
www.highlandoutdoors.co.uk
0845 099 0252
Leica, Bushnell, Weaver
www.shootingsports.
edgarbrothers.com
01625 613177

light is concerned, the lenses and, just as importantly, the coatings used start to spread the gap. Maintaining clear point of aim on quarry emerging from dingy cover when you are in bright conditions is a real test for scopes, even more so where the sun may be shining towards you and causing flare.

When you really start to research the complexities of optics, you learn about factors that, when comparing glass side by side in identical scenarios, really highlight where your money has gone. For example, when viewing a target on a bright day with the sun shining towards you, can you see without the lenses flaring out, or reflections off the external surfaces interfering with your view? Do you notice colours fringing around the external profile of an animal as they are distorted through a process called chromatic aberration, in which differing frequencies (colours) of light refract through lenses with different points of focus and cause halo effects? On the finest glass, red, green and blue are all corrected for, but cheaper optics often show up the green fringing first. All those thousands of hours spent developing closely guarded lens-coating secrets are well represented in these conditions, and the fact that manufacturer 'A' uses twinned compound lenses where manufacturer 'B' uses single lenses isn't the kind of fact you notice looking out of a shop window at a telegraph pole across the road.

Don't assume more magnification will improve matters. It can be a false perception that increased size is clearer. Perception of colours from one human to the next is very personal – my own left and right eyes see small differences, so it it no surprise to encounter the same among other shooters.

Parallax correction is present in all optics. In some it is fixed at 100/200 metres; others offer adjustability. On a hunting scope, the general rule for centrefire scopes is that 12x is about the maximum magnification that can be used before parallax (although ever present) becomes noticeable. The addition of its internal adjustability adds further cost. Recent testing on a 15x scope with otherwise superb image quality, but parallax fixed at 200 metres, was slightly out of focus at 100 metres when zeroing. Parallax is a complex subject in itself but essentially, as well as allowing the user to obtain clear focus at the intended magnification and range (more so with higher mag), it focuses the image on the same plane as the reticle, and keeps the two in sync to prevent any misalignment of the eye effectively shifting the point of impact. High magnification and longer ranges amplify the significance. You won't make a parallax error with a slightly fuzzy

4x image at 40 yards on a rabbit with a 6x scope, but that 400-yard crow with a 20x scope might easily evade you if an unrealised parallax error was involved.

Externally dialling target turrets and the newer hunting-specific designs with calculated ranges add further options to the equation, but that is another article in itself. Many buyers think recoil is the big killer of scopes, but repeated mechanical adjustments made to any scope not really intended for repetitive dialling will wear internal mechanisms, so be aware. Warranties on optics are subtly changing as the trend to dial scopes for more precision grows. Size and weight are factors to consider, and compact controls are certainly preferable on a pure hunting rifle. There is no point destroying all the gunmaker's elegant workmanship with unnecessary optical features and weight. The option to remain at fixed magnification and keep everything simple is tempting!

Choosing a scope at any budget should be a well-researched task. Anybody criticising scopes from lower price ranges is wrong to do so as the facilities they offer are amazing considering the technology and precision involved. Likewise, scopes at the premium end of the market are worth their cost. Although the improvement is hard to see when peering through the glass in a daytime shop, those last 10 minutes of hunting time at dusk may be the difference between an £80 stalk offering a shot or not, and when you multiply that throughout the life of a scope, it is money well invested. Optics made in the US and Asia have rapidly caught up with the technologies in European brands, often outpacing their marketing inertia when it comes to newer mechanical specification choices, but they aren't quite there with the glass yet. What they do offer is fantastic value for money. Warranties are a fact that should be observed carefully, as some companies offer quibble-free lifetime guarantees where some brands only offer two years. It reflects their confidence in the products they make and their suitability to the intended task, so it's reassuring in the long term. The world is alive with subjective opinions, but factual knowledge has never been easier to research. Read around the technical facts of the subjects and then apply those facts objectively to the optics you question. Even the big names in Europe aren't afraid to admit some of their glass is a little oriental, so keep an open mind!

Chris Parkin, freelance shooting journalist

The No. 60 reticle: Precise for daylight but still illuminated

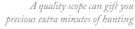
A quality scope can gift you precious extra minutes of hunting

MODERATOR MANIA

T he question of which is the best sound moderator regularly floats around, with a lot of hearsay and subjective opinion inevitably following. Side-by-side testing and full acoustic monitoring to give objective comparisons are hard to organise, but those of us who have shot a lot of them on a wide variety of calibres can still notice a few trends. When I started shooting, sound moderators were in their infancy to sporting shots, and getting a variation for one was not guaranteed, but the ongoing tide of health and safety has overcome this situation. Where a target shooter used to have no chance of getting a mod, it is now common to see them among 'tactical' rifle fans, and it seems a foxing rifle is missing something if not modded. Similarly, deer stalking has seen an increase in sound moderator use. This growth in use has led to many new models, styles and thought processes to fulfil our requirements of a mod. It has proven some models excellent, many ok and a few certainly to be avoided. Most importantly, it has brought our real requirements of a moderator to more detailed attention.

Baffle build: A lightweight aluminium structure with stainless steel at points of extreme risk

SOUND MODERATOR NEEDS

So what does a sound moderator do? Most of us think noise attenuation is the primary requirement; recoil reduction is also a factor, but what about durability? It certainly polarises opinion. When you fire a rifle, a fast, hot jet of gas comes bursting out of the muzzle, creating a lot of noise or 'muzzle blast'. This jet reacts with the atmosphere to create recoil in exactly the same way a jet engine propels a plane.

So for foxing, what are our primary needs? Moderating sound for us as well as for residents within earshot would be the first consideration. Weight is not such a big issue if you are foxing from a vehicle, but durability is certainly key. A foxing rifle is likely to be shot regularly, brought into the house and stored late at night in a hurry, perhaps forgotten until its next outing.

Compare this with a stalking rifle: in a single-shot environment, right or wrong as it is, we can mostly forgive ourselves the odd open-air boom now and again, but mitigating surrounding animals' reactions to their suddenly immobile companion can be very useful when culling herding deer. In woodland, minimising recoil can help the shooter spot their bullet impact, and when close to heavy cover, it is certainly helpful to have a starting idea of the type of hit and primary injury you have inflicted on a deer you may spend hours tracking. Viewing shot reaction can be extremely valuable.

Lastly, a stalking rifle may well be put away during the day or evening, allowed to warm up to room temperature, be cared for before storage and see a significantly lower round count through its life. So it's likely to be less of a strain on durability.

A quick note of caution: always take your moderator off the rifle before storage. Condensation forms and will rot a barrel faster than you can click your fingers – be warned.

MATERIALS

Having defined specific needs, we can look at the materials and construction style. Moderators can come in Parkerised steel, stainless steel, titanium, as a composite build using aluminium/steel combinations, or an entire carbon fibre unit. Choosing a mod that can be dismantled for cleaning or one that is welded shut and left forever depends on your requirements and its expected lifespan. On a foxing rifle, I would personally use a slightly heavier steel mod. On a stalking rig, an aluminium mod with stainless baffles or baffle centres seems to fit the bill well; although a little lighter in weight, it is the common solution for low round count and strip-down maintenance.

To debunk a few myths, a moderator prevents the jet of gas creating excessive noise and recoil by slowing the pressure release from the muzzle. The jet is made to swirl, expand and diminish before it hits the external atmosphere, and expend the momentum that causes the gun to recoil rearward. This is where volume always helps, but the simple fact is, the gas is going forwards: weight for weight, an end-of-barrel mod will always minimise noise and recoil better than a reflex design. Moderators can get a bit long and wand-like, but there are some seriously compact and low-weight units out there performing well above their stature.

BRAKE AND MOD

I dispute the claims of manufacturers who suggest you can call whatever baffles or internal blast arrangements of the mod's internals a muzzle 'brake'. A muzzle brake works by expelling gas rapidly, directly to the external atmosphere, thereby reducing the jet directed forward, and expending its energy radially or laterally in complete equilibrium, sometimes rearwards to reverse the jet's momentum. It won't work inside a sealed pressure vessel. It might look like a brake and it may cause gas swirling and expansion to depressurise within the tube, but it isn't a brake – it's part of a moderator.

For the target or tactical shooters who want a mod for range use, you can get a brake that is screwed to the end of the barrel, working in the usual fashion,

The Hardy mod is a model that suits stalkers well

If your mod can be dismantled, treat the fouling with care and reassemble it tightly

MODERATORS: WHAT'S ON THE MARKET

ASE Utra, A-Tec and BR–Tuote Reflex
www.jacksonrifles.com
Hardy Sound Moderators
www.riflecraft.co.uk
Third Eye Tactical Spartan
www.thirdeyetactical.com
Brugger & Thomet
www.vikingarms.com
PES/MAE moderators
www.jmsarms.com
Sonic moderators
www.highlandoutdoors.co.uk

and a paired mod will then screw over the brake, giving sound reduction performance. However, make no mistake: the brake has become nothing more than a mounting spigot. It no longer ejects to the atmosphere. Of course, some intelligently designed mods have more than one exit hole up front to allow further gas discharge away from the direct bore line, but these are exits for gases already reduced in pressure, not the initial blast wave. I'd pick a heavy stainless steel mod for durability with great sound suppression – I wouldn't want to strip it or risk anything being loose internally.

MODERATORS OVER TIME

A solid mod, regardless of material, will eventually rot or burn away. It is exposed to high temperature gases at extreme speeds and pressures that will 'cut' the surfaces and remove coatings. Some materials will suffer more than others. A mod that can be dismantled for cleaning won't have any corrosion flakes tinkling around inside it like a steel mod will. On the other hand, until the day it dies, a welded mod won't come loose, and any slack in the components of a strippable mod can cause accuracy issues as vibration disturbs the harmonics of your barrel. Most manufacturers suggest checking that the mod is fully tightened when hot and expanding. That way, when cool, it will only get tighter so should cause no problem at either end of the temperature scale. A quick blast of WD40 or such is often recommended but regularly overdone, and the first shot afterwards is a huge blast of white smoke – a terrible smell. I have seen one 'enthusiastic lubricator' actually achieve full detonation and a burst mod, thankfully without injury. Chances are, your 'cold bore shot' will be off zero too. If you must, be very sparing.

Modular construction means you can change specific parts to suit your rifle

Manufacturing technology has changed significantly, so where we once saw only pressed steel tubes welded together, almost semi-disposable items from military backgrounds, CNC machining has allowed combinations of materials specified to suit individual localised needs within the moderator. For example, you can use a lighter weight aluminium tube and end caps with stainless steel baffles to minimise gas cutting, aluminium baffles with stainless centres to reduce weight, or increase the number of baffles. Baffles are now machined with such intricacy that designers can explore more ideas of fluid dynamics to disperse the jet. Also, as computer modelling becomes more accessible, ideas will evolve further. Modular construction means one moderator can fit several rifles regardless of thread size, or can be adapted to a new rifle. Baffles were once offered in .25 or .30 to cover all sporting calibres, but some are now specific for .17, .20 and .22 to minimise all noise possible. Magnum calibres are catered for with .30. Moderators are available for .338 and .408, even the 'fifty', but these are a far cry from the .223 foxing rifle's needs. The increasing market for moderators and brakes has led to more companies screw-cutting their barrels at the time of manufacture, helpfully avoiding the proof issue that still rears its head occasionally.

Chris Parkin, freelance shooting journalist

Ultrasonic cleaners will shift powder residue

Photo: James Marchington

STALKING CLOTHING

To start with, I always live by the infantier's mantra, "Look after your feet and you will go a long way." Good, well-fitting and preferably breathable boots, which are capable of standing up to the variable British weather, are essential for extended stalking outings.

Hill roe will need a sturdy boot such as the Black Islander No Scratch boot and the 9in Graphite boot. These boots have a number of unique qualities – the all-leather boots are covered with a unique man-made waterproof, yet breathable, new-concept rubberised fabric, which is bonded onto the leather upper and sole, preventing water from entering the boot at the seam. They also feature a Windex waterproof and breathable liner, lightweight, rust-free eyelets, rubber toe and are shod with the time-served Vibram sole. Additionally they are surprisingly lightweight for a rugged boot, and are my personal choice for most stalking scenarios.

On the low ground, especially when foot stalking as opposed to high seat shooting, a lightweight, thin-soled boot makes all the difference when it comes to not giving away your position. A thinner sole will let you feel more with your feet. I have a pair of Danner Jackal II GTX XCR 7in tactical hiking boots from Edgar Brothers – they are superb for this kind of work.

As editor of *Sporting Rifle* magazine, I often test a variety of stalking clothing, and most of it is fit for purpose, but you do get what you pay for. For years I have been a big fan of Deerhunter, who supply superb, practical hunting garments at a reasonable

Harkila Prohunter: Real top-end stuff

price. I also have a Harkila Prohunter suit that is exceptionally tough, waterproof and breathable – but it is heavy. My first choice for the past two years has been the Deerhunter Recon suit. It has an innovative pixelated camo design using shades of green, brown and grey. It is superb, breathable and waterproof; the cut of the jacket and trousers is perfect for stalking and crawling without unnecessary tension on the legs or shoulders. The only small criticism I have is the slight noise it makes – though no more so than many other contenders – but Deerhunter has since produced a new version called the Cumberland that is virtually silent. This is difficult to achieve with any garment containing a membrane, but the brown fleece outer material makes it virtually silent without losing any of its breathability or water-repelling qualities. It is set to be a winner, of that I'm sure.

For a long time I used Deerhunter's Game Stalker suit. It is a light and flexible anorak, trouser and cap, perfectly suited for traditional stalking in Realtree AP camouflage. This pattern is especially suited for the autumn and winter, but I find it perfectly acceptable for spring and summer too. The suit comes in the soft, yet durable Deer-Tex stretch membrane material, which is extremely comfortable is wind and waterproof and comes complete with Velcro-adjustable cuffs, knee-length leg zippers, elasticated waistband and plenty of pockets. The snap-pull adjustable hood is kept out of sight and in place when not in use by two discreet magnets. A hidden zippered neck pocket contains an integral and practical mosquito net facemask. Regardless of where and when you go hunting, you can rest assured that the combination of Realtree AP and manufacturing quality provides the camouflage and reliability that I have come to expect from Deerhunter. Their Ram jacket has pretty much become the industry standard in stalking circles.

I use Black Islander Deluxe gaiters, as they are simply the best on the market, a view shared by most of Scotland's hill keepers. They are exceptional. A lightweight, waterproof but breathable soft upper shell is complemented by a hardwearing Cordura lower shell ankle piece that will defy the roughest of heather. A heavy-duty front zipper (often overlooked by other manufacturers) enables simplicity of use with Velcro cover flap. Further features are a robust double-riveted large steel lace hook and pop-studded tie top. These gaiters have been my choice for more than a decade.

Remember, quality kit fit for purpose will not only make your stalking outings more comfortable and increase your success rates, on the hill or in other remote areas, they might make the difference between life and death.

Washing stalking clothing correctly shouldn't be overlooked. Perfumed washing powder and fabric conditioners are of course counterproductive. I soak my bloodied clothing in cold water and then put it through the machine on a warm wash without any additional powder or conditioner. There are a number of scentless washing products on the market aimed at hunters and I have tried them. All I can say is that American bow hunters, who of course have to get very close to their game, swear by these products. I'm not against them – it's more that I forget to buy them, and a cold soak followed by a warm wash works for me. **PC**

The author in tried-and-tested Deerhunter stalking gear

THE RIGHT RIFLE?

By *Andrew Venables*

Clients of my company, WMS Firearms Training, sometimes arrive wanting to improve their lethality as hunters with rifles and scopes that were never made for hunting. It is not surprising that some shooters buy the wrong equipment: there are many products on the market and the media, advertising, product placement, reviews and websites all try to influence us to buy what manufacturers, importers and dealers want us to buy. The result is that we can end up with kit that doesn't suit us or our shooting, which can be an expensive mistake.

For shooters who want to hunt live quarry, a good rifle is indispensable. The essence of such a firearm is one that can be carried comfortably into the countryside and wild places where deer, antelope and other game are found. The most important factors to consider when deciding which rifle to buy are length, weight and balance.

This is especially pertinent when hunting in the mountains or highlands of Scotland, where every kilogram matters, and in woodland stalking where ease of handling and balance are key. All three factors are also crucial for shooting foxes, taking on wild boar in the forests of Europe and hunting plains game in Africa.

LENGTH

Let's look at what makes a good sporting rifle in more detail. From my perspective, 40 years of experience in the field has made me appreciate well-balanced rifles in

modest calibres with barrels of not more than 51cm for hunting. I also like removable magazines that can be topped up from above too, and effective moderators that don't add undue length or weight. On length, I don't want the rifle barrel to stick up way over my head when shoulder-slung, so a rifle of under 110cm including moderator is good.

WEIGHT

Weight-wise, I am looking for under 4kg when fitted with scope, sling and moderator. A great test in the gun shop is to hold the rifle straight out at arm's length, in your left hand if you are right-handed, or vice versa. If you can't hold it at all, the rifle is a bench gun; if you can hold it for 30 seconds, it is a good, general-purpose hunting rifle; if you can hold it for 60 seconds – and it can hit beer mats at 300 metres – then it's a real mountain rifle.

A good rifle shouldn't weigh you down...

The Scout specification of rifle, as designed and promoted by the late Colonel Jeff Cooper of Gunsite, is a good choice for hunters. The original Scout spec was for an acceptably accurate rifle, at less than 1 metre long and weighing under 3kg (not including scope and moderator), used primarily for hunting. Today's Steyr Scout and Ruger Gunsite Scout are prime examples, with Savage and Mossberg also producing good Scout-style rifles. In addition, most of the major rifle manufacturers produce lightweight rifles for hunting, and also offer a choice of rifles with light to medium-weight barrels from 46-53cm. As long as these barrels are fully free-floated, they rarely shoot badly.

As an aside, don't obsess about shooting tiny groups – any rifle that shoots between 2cm and 5cm three-shot groups at 100 metres with the usual range of factory ammo is good enough. Furthermore, most centre-fire rifles, scopes and ammunition for sale today, once zeroed, can shoot groups like this out to 200 metres from stable positions, such as prone and off benches. The standard Winchester, Remington, Steyr, Tikka, CZ/BRNO, Sako and other hunting rifles I own can also shoot good three-shot groups at ranges where no one should be attempting to shoot anything with a pulse. However, they don't do this when the shooter is breathless, tired, under pressure and struggling to manage the weight of the rifle while setting up sticks or finding a suitable position.

..should be paired with a suitable scope...

Hence, an over-heavy rifle in the field is detrimental to lethality and saves more game than it harvests by slowing the shooter down. In my experience, shooting from standing, kneeling, sitting, leaning against trees and from vehicles is much easier with regular to light hunting rifles and genuinely difficult with long and heavy-barrelled overdressed bench guns.

Interestingly, some the custom rifle makers are now embracing the creation of lighter rifles and we are starting to see some exquisite, light and accurate rifles with barrels as short as 41cm. It is worth noting, however, that while some calibres work well with short barrels, others don't. For example, magnum calibres, or necked-down calibres like .243Win and 25.06 need between 51-

66cm to burn all the powder and perform properly. I have a .243Win with a 48cm barrel that loses over 10 per cent velocity with 90-100gn bullets. I also own a .308Win with the same length barrel that loses a maximum of 3 per cent, which is inconsequential. So remember: long, heavy barrels are for shooting ranges and long distances where every last metre per second counts. You will be firing hundreds of rounds and you have to carry the rifle no more than 50 metres.

BALANCE

A rifle that balances well will place equal weight in each hand when held in regular shooting positions. As with a good shotgun, the rifle barrel will point naturally at the target and not feel like a dead weight in the hands. My Blaser R8, Browning A Bolt, Steyr Scout, BRNO 602 .375 H&H and 30-year-old Sako Vixen all point and swing really well thanks to being balanced. They also shoot accurately both prone and off the shooting bench. Balance is a very personal thing; what may feel balanced to one person may not to another, so pick up rifles and see how they feel – you'll know when one suits you.

SCOPES

Scopes that work best for me when hunting are high quality and either fixed six-power or zoom scopes in the ranges of 1.5-6, 3-9, or maybe 3-12 or 4-16 for longer ranges. High magnification and small fields of view are more a hindrance than help when shooting live game. There is a trend for very high magnification telescopic sights in the 10-50 power range but using the 20-50 power range will result in an increasingly dim picture, rapidly shrinking field of view and the likely loss of target during recoil. Shooting live quarry demands good light gathering, a wide field of view for safety and the ability to keep the quarry in view if at all possible during recoil and while reloading in the shoulder.

Hunt animals with hunting scopes, and use the big stuff for F-Class and long-range target shooting.

KEEP IT SIMPLE

I own rifles and scopes of many different types. My 'go guns' – the ones I rely on and take hunting – are the handy ones, a pleasure to carry, reliable, easy to mount and work with, and accurate enough to do the job every time as long as I do my bit properly. They are regular calibres – the ones most gun shops carry ammunition for. For hunting, keep it simple and rely on proven products – but do have fun target shooting with bench guns, 'Hubble' telescopes and exotic new calibres too.

Book your training session with Andrew Venables: 01974 831869, www. wmsfirearmstraining.com

...and should suit a variety of situations

DOMINIC GRIFFITH

Dominic Griffith is without question one of the most knowledgeable stalkers and authoritative deer managers still practising in Great Britain today. A dedicated deer manager, Dominic has been extremely generous with his hard-won knowledge, always willing to share his vast experience and passion for roe with his fellow enthusiasts.

Today he is perhaps best known as an incredibly thorough trophy measurer. Cutting his teeth with the late, great Kenneth Whitehead and the renowned Richard Prior, he achieved massive respect as a CIC measurer before going on to launch the successful BASC measuring service, which he still heads.

He is also a board director (trustee) of both the British Deer Society and the Deer Initiative, and is responsible for managing the deer on 15,000 acres in Hampshire. Dominic has a wide and continuing involvement in deer management training at all levels. He is known as an expert in collaborative culling techniques.

As well as in regular articles and trophy reports in the sporting press, Dominic has put his wisdom on paper in his book *Deer Management in the UK*, which quickly became known as one of the definitive works on UK deer stalking. The book fascinatingly and authoritatively imparts his clear enthusiasm for deer and in particular roe, their habits, and ways to analyse and improve their quality. As far as roe experts go, there are very few who surpass Dominic Griffith.

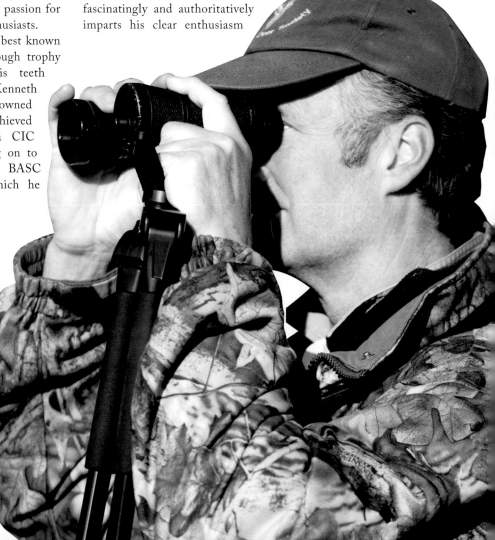

WHAT MAKES A GOOD BUCK?

Taken over the past 20 or more years, the annual variation in quality of roebucks remains an enigma that captivates and puzzles all roe enthusiasts alike. We've had some great years (most notably 1991, 2002 and 2006) and some shockers too (few will forget a miserable 2007). But why is there such a variation from year to year? With many theories put forward, it is worth examining what may or may not be the case.

Surely the most compelling argument must be quite simply food and shelter. Provided the buck has a sufficient food intake to ensure a surplus to put into his antler development, and provided that the weather conditions are no worse than average, then surely he will flourish? Sadly even this simple concept has flaws – what do we mean by good weather? I remember when I started stalking professionally we used to reckon that the deer 'needed a bit of snow on their backs', which 'made them work for their food' to create good antlers. Maybe what we meant by this was enough cold to kill or suppress the ecto-parasites, taken alongside the natural association between a cold, dry winter as against a mild, wet and windy one.

Add to that pot the concept that Vitamin D from a winter of relatively high winter sunshine hours might also benefit calcium development. Clearly it takes

Photo: Shutterstock

less energy to simply keep warm as compared to keeping dry and warm, so the former ensures surplus nutrient for antler development. As for winter sunshine and Vitamin D, it seems to make sense. I wish it were that simple, but recent years have tended to bring dry, cold winters, and without the results that might have been predicted.

I've seen some truly awful years. Low sunshine hours, the wettest Novembers and Decembers on record, cold snaps without the associated clarity of air that normally follows snow. In these situations it seems the roe will have no chance – but who knows?

Photo: Andy Lee

If food is important, and to some degree it must be, then surely high protein food must be a key component. The most common source of high protein food is sourced in pheasant feed – predominantly in wheat. Where roe have access to high protein agricultural crops and in particular to a commercial pheasant shoot, they certainly thrive. This explains why central Southern England and the central agricultural belt of Scotland regularly produce the finest heads, but it does not explain the annual fluctuation in that quality. That said, I concede that one estate I know was formerly famous for its roe quality when at the same time it supported an extremely intensive commercial shoot. The shoot was closed down some years ago, and there seems little doubt that this is reflected to some extent in an apparent current overall reduction in roe quality.

Some say that access to the best 'territory' within the stalking area is the most significant aspect of antler development, and that may well be true but, again, it fails to explain this annual variation within overall good quality. Furthermore, trials in the UK with salt licks or feed supplements are inconclusive, the roe being inherent browsers and having sufficient natural browse here to satisfy them.

What is the secret behind roebucks like these?

Richard Prior, universally considered to be the greatest authority on roe, was interested in a theory which was proposed by the Duke of Bavaria that the most important aspect of a great buck was its birth year. So instead of examining the winter immediately preceding the year of antler development, we should instead be examining whether the buck was born in one of these great birth years when presumably all the kids had a better than average start to their lives. This is an absolutely fascinating argument, and one which I have long considered. I have no idea if it may be the nemesis, but I am worried about the association in that it fails to tally with how bucks often develop in the first year. When selecting bucks as yearlings it is common practice to select on antler development and many stalkers will quite reasonably shoot their cull of yearlings simply from those with antlers 'below the ears'.

However, the records show that such bucks are often the heaviest, and indeed that just as often those 'wonderful yearling six pointers' are frequently found to be the skinniest and weakest in body condition. Nowadays my own view is to cull yearlings based on body condition alone, almost regardless of antler development.

Other eminent roe experts have suggested that the quality of the bucks is solely down to the quality of the dam (the mother doe). If this is the case then sadly there is little we can do to influence the outcome. It does not seem a convincing argument to me, but cannot be discounted.

One thing is true: the number and range of quality roe is increasing. Twenty years ago, despite roe being present in Yorkshire and Cumbria, bucks of medal class were virtually unknown. Today both counties contribute regularly to the annual reviews.

The argument of genetics versus environment remains unclear, although there seems little doubt that the roe of Hampshire derived from two separate sources, one from Sussex and one from Dorset. The Sussex buck was always identifiable as a narrow, heavy and well-pearled trophy. The Dorset buck tended to be wider, more regular and less pearled. It seems that Hampshire, un-colonised until the early 70s, may have benefited from some hybrid vigour, inheriting the best characteristics of both sources.

The Norfolk roe definitely have smaller skulls, but is this down to genetic or environmental factors? Norfolk and Suffolk now both contribute the occasional trophy to the annual reviews, though they rarely did a decade ago. But overall quality is one thing, the annual variation is quite another.

In another 25 years I would love to be in a position to answer this conundrum but, in the meantime, the only influence we can have is in the basics of overall quality. We cannot choose which county we live in, but that is clearly an important factor. We cannot necessarily influence the farming practices, but would hope for mixed cropping (with a bias towards winter wheat) and low livestock levels. We cannot necessarily influence the forestry policy, but would hope for mixed farm woodland with good understorey, plenty of edge and within an environment of mixed species and age class. If there is a pheasant shoot, so much the better as that will ensure no shortage of winter food and cover and the possibility of some high protein supplement.

For our part, we must allow our bucks to live a stress-free existence and where possible employ low pressure management techniques. Finally, and most importantly, we must allow them to get old enough to develop to their greatest potential. **DG**

Trophy heads aren't just luck...

...a sound management plan is required to create them

Dominic Griffith

HEAD START

At the start of the buck season, many roe stalkers will be eagerly anticipating another spring and summer in search of their bucks. Will the weather be conducive to magnificent dawns and balmy evenings, or will we be cursing the cold, withering in the wind and ruing the endless rain?

Others' thoughts turn to trophies. Whether you are looking for the weakest to cull, a bizarre curiosity or that wonderful old medal buck, the one matter that cannot fail to stimulate the imagination is: What will be the relative size of their antlers this year? Will it be a great year or an indifferent one? We always used to say you needed winter snow to grow big bucks, but I know that other stalkers are worried that the cold winter will have depressed antler growth. We all watch our bucks in velvet when they begin to show their potential from mid-January, and come late February we might begin to get excited about some of the better ones, but until the velvet is off you simply cannot tell just how thick and dense the remaining antler will be.

There seems to be a great deal of confusion regarding the classification of trophies. This has led some stalkers' trophies to be classified 'un-measurable' – which I take to mean 'unclassified', as despite this description the trophy has actually been attributed a measurement. So let us be clear. All hard antlers can be measured, although some throw up greater or lesser challenges. Trophies taken in velvet clearly cannot be measured as the rules apply to the measurement of the bone itself.

Otherwise, roe trophies are divided into 'typical' and 'non-typical', but even that leaves some room for argument. The rule we used to stick to was that if the trophy could be dipped to achieve a volume measurement, then multi-point heads would be classified as 'typical'. If the antler protruded in such a way that it could not be completely immersed in water, then what could be measured would be measured but the trophy would have to be classified as non-typical. In either case, the appropriate medal could be issued, although official medals were not normally issued to non-typical trophies.

Then there were 'Baillie' heads, a description that has stuck since Major the Hon. Peter Baillie's trophy of 1974. This must be in many respects the most important head in the history of trophy assessment, as it is a benchmark in what became accepted or rejected for official measurement. Measured in the UK as a world record but subsequently disqualified by international judges, it took the epithet of a 'Baillie Monster'. Although huge, it exhibited unusual and excessive bone growth with 'the appearance of poured and hardened cement' around

Photo: Andy Lee

the coronet and extending to the underside of the eye socket. International judges decided that this made it non-typical and unfair to judge against 'normal' trophies.

At the time it was unique, but over the years more have been presented and there are now at least 20 of its type known to exist among collections. Why they develop remains a mystery, but they are associated with areas where very high-protein food is in abundance (typically low-ground pheasant shoots). More than half a dozen have passed through my hands over the years, and my only comment is that if a 'Baillie Monster' were to be judged a world record it is certain that no 'normal' trophy could ever retake that title. Today the classification appears to have been blurred, with many clearly Baillie-type trophies apparently being recognised for official measurement. I believe that it is important to recognise any excessive bone growth on the skull and eye sockets 'with the appearance of poured hardened cement', and to classify them correctly.

Then there are the so-called 'mossed heads', of which several have been recorded over the years. Perfectly measurable but non-typical, there appears to be massive confusion as to their provenance and status. None have ever been shot in that form, and nearly all have been found dead. Surely this in itself must speak volumes. I had always suspected that they were no more than the remnants of 'perruques' after the buck had died and the organic matter rotted from their antlers, and this was proved to be the case when Marco Pierre White shot his enormous perruque in 2010.

A perruque head describes antler growth that has been starved of testosterone. The antler continues to grow under its protective velvet covering until the buck is blinded or the skull splits. Those surviving into late summer inevitably succumb to fly-strike and die. However, the taxidermist Colin Dunton has developed a unique method of setting up a perruque that leaves the original perruque intact and removes the remaining antler as a boiled trophy. These remains – the so-called 'mossed heads' – are completely measurable, but must remain classified as 'non-typical'.

Freshly boiled, or very dry, they remain more porous than normal antlers and will therefore absorb water quicker. Indeed, the absorption rate of normal antler is extremely slow – so slow that it is not recognisable during the usual process of measurement. Thus the volume measurement of a mossed head must be taken smartly in one short dip. It is nevertheless incorrect to describe them as heavily 'pearled', as this shows a complete misunderstanding of the nature of the 'perruque'.

But are some of the really great trophies 'normal'? Consider the existing Swedish record, or indeed Michael Langmead's 1971 buck, which held the record as the biggest UK roe buck for 35 years. Giant? Yes. Multi-point? Yes. Normal in skull development? Yes. But typical of the species? Well, they are not average six-pointers, certainly, but they differ only in the way that a great athlete may not quite have the same physique as the rest of us. Let's not allow the boundaries to be crossed, because that will make nonsense of 50 years of record-keeping in the UK, and let's make sure that those making the judgements really have sufficient understanding of the species to make those judgements. **DG**

Christopher Usher's Baillie-esque Yorkshire record?

A top trophy shot by a client of David Virtue

EFFECTIVE STALKING

Photo above:
Brian Phipps

Photo right:
Andy Lee

The old adage 'practice makes perfect' applies as much to deer stalking as it does to any other skill or pastime. With practice, we come to know the ground, the deer, their behaviour and their feeding patterns. With roe deer, an amateur would generally get to know how the deer use the ground after just a couple of seasons' experience and would then reckon on one selective cull per three outings. A professional will have to do better and work towards an average of one selective cull per outing. Some years ago my own average through November was an average of 1.4 roe per outing.

With fallow, this average is dramatically reduced to the extent that it makes little sense for a single person to try to achieve the cull alone. In many circumstances the only way that fallow can be stalked efficiently is for at least two people to work together, and even then success will rarely match that experienced with roe.

As our personal skills improve, the most significant advance in success rate comes in 'timing'. Much has to do with being predictive, and understanding the techniques used by the individual species to feed. Muntjac, for example, tend to dart around the forest, pausing briefly to snatch a bite here and there. They are a small quarry, often obscured by the understory. It is therefore essential to observe their direction of movement, and to try to predict where they will move to. Then, if you see a clear area, you can get the rifle up and waiting so if the deer passes through that area, may be offering an opportunity for a shot.

The roe, on the other hand, is a much more sedentary feeder, typically taking a few paces between each bite and stopping to look around in between. Shots should not be taken while a roe's head is lowered to feed, as the vital organs are pressed into the stomach. However, when it throws the head up to look around before resuming its motion through the forest, this gives the perfect opportunity for a shot. The whole procedure becomes a rhythmic and predictable pattern of movement into which the chance of a shot is readily planned and eventually becomes second nature to you as a stalker.

Another factor that becomes increasingly important is the effective use of daylight. Many of us, often under pressure from clients, force ourselves into the illogical situation of entering the forest before dawn.

In fact, the records prove that this is a poor use of time, and often reduces success through filling the forest with unnecessary human scent before the deer are even visible. Furthermore, having repeatedly risen too early, you are then tired after 2-3 hours and inclined to return for breakfast – at precisely the time when the records show the roe to be at their most active.

In a sample of 2,000 consecutively stalked deer (excluding does culled in movements) including 1,180 does and 820 bucks, the results will come as a surprise to many. Of the bucks culled in the morning, 90 per cent were shot between

Photo:
Andy Lee

5.15am and 8.30am, with a clear peak around 7am. Although 18 of the 820 bucks were shot at very first light, it accounts for only 2 per cent of the total cull, and one has to ask oneself whether it was worth 'busting a gut' to get up so early for them, especially as there is every chance that many of them might have been shot at more normal times. Furthermore, particularly in April when cold north-easterly winds frequently blight the early signs of spring, bucks are often more active after 8am. I believe that many stalkers are tiring and returning home just as the deer are beginning to become active. Surprisingly, midday rut stalking accounted for only about 2.5 per cent of the total.

During the evening buck stalking period, 91 per cent were shot between 7pm and 9.30pm with a clear peak 8pm. So the morning has a three-hour effective period, but the evening only a 2.5-hour peak of activity. Perhaps the most interesting bit of information, which surprised me as the counting progressed, is that the evening/morning success ratio is almost precisely even at 51 to 49 per cent.

Turning to the morning doe cull, 87 per cent of all does culled were shot between 6.30am and 9am, with a clear peak around 8am. The later morning, however, is significantly more productive than with the bucks. This has much to do with the feeding activity of roe does in late winter, when in certain conditions they can be active at all times of the day. Note also that people always talk of restricted winter stalking time, but here is the proof that the effective 2.5-hour period between 6.30am and 9am is a full one hour less than the equivalent effective summer buck stalking time.

In the evening, however, there is some compensation in that the effective stalking period is slightly more extended and more evenly distributed than for the bucks. It lasts from 3pm to 5.45pm – during this time 94 per cent of all does were shot, and there was no clear peak hour.

One might ask why anyone would ever stalk alone when collaborative culling is so much more productive. More and more stalkers are realising that collaboration at one level or another has an exponential effect on their returns. Two people stalking or sitting more than doubles the net success, while 10 on the same area exceeds even that.

Of course this method of culling is not for everyone, especially if as a recreational stalker you wish to enjoy each and every outing yourself. But when you get behind and have a significant cull to achieve in a short time, consider collaborating with your neighbours and they will be sure to reciprocate and the object achieved. **DG**

You might not need to get up at 3am to grass that buck. Photo: Brian Phipps

SELECTION

While the doe cull can often present a challenge, the buck cull is a relatively relaxed affair. The season is long, the days are long, and the weather is more conducive to spending time in the woods.

Although many stalkers like to get out on 1 April, I believe they would do better to wait. There are several factors that influence stalking success: temperature, air pressure, moon phase, wind, rain, availability of feed, undergrowth, and relative territorial activity among the bucks.

In April, new grazing starts to become available but it is often cold, the wind bites, and territorial behaviour becomes subdued. Stalking bucks in those circumstances can be a depressing affair. In May, the average temperature is higher, browse becomes plentiful, and territorial behaviour intensifies.

Stalker and quarry operate on completely different time, space, and sensory planes. The temporal aspect of stalking, which is critical to your chances of coming across the right buck at the right time and in the right place to permit a safe shot, is limiting enough. Add the deer's different use of its senses, and its different understanding of topography (where, for example, thick bramble bushes do not represent a barrier), then it is perhaps extraordinary that stalker and quarry ever come together.

To increase the chances of colliding with your buck, it helps if he is moving around. In late May, the bucks are at their most active outside the rut, and are readily stalked despite the growth of ground cover. I have spent many miserable days stalking in April trying to 'beat the cover', but enjoyed unprecedented success in late May. Furthermore, it just does not seem right to be stalking a buck in its coat change, and with uncoloured antlers.

Selection of bucks to be included in the cull often produces fierce debate. In my opinion there are only two important criteria. Firstly you have got to have some idea of what is on the ground in spring (so you have got to spend some time doing a census), and secondly you have got to ensure the cull removes a representative slice of the population, targeting the older

This is where the census and cull plan come together.
Photo: Flickr

Antler condition and positiong can indicate a buck's age.
Photo: Andy Lovel

Photo: Andy Lovel

age classes, sparing the young middle-aged (or improving) bucks, and taking the required number of yearlings.

The important points are to fix the number of bucks to be culled, to avoid shooting the younger middle-aged bucks, and to be aware of the mistakes you are bound to make. Longer-term success will rely upon your ability to make as few ageing mistakes as possible, and this is something which comes only with years of experience, and even then is not infallible.

Ageing mistakes lead to a cull that is essentially a random slice of the population – but as long as it is truly random, it is unlikely that long-term mismanagement will occur. Unfortunately too many stalkers set aside their mistakes and continue the cull without amendment to the cull plan. If you have stalked buck 'A', shot buck 'B' by mistake and found that he was not as good or as old as you had hoped, then I'm afraid that either Buck 'A' has to be spared for the season, or if he is so old that he will die anyway, then you must make a commensurate reduction in next year's cull.

I have found the most useful live indicator to be the angle of the coronet. Where the coronets are flat, obvious and close together, the buck is almost certainly young. Where the coronets are sloping in the form of a 'roof', and positioned apart, then the buck is almost certainly old. This may be difficult to see at 100 metres in poor light, but it is amazing how few stalkers check the bases of the antlers, instead getting carried away by height and bright points, which can be misleading.

Coat change is another useful indicator – old bucks tend to retain their winter coats into late May. Gait is also important: unstressed, an old buck will hold its head low and patrol his territory with quiet confidence, while a younger buck will be constantly alert and looking around him, holding the head high. Sharp white tines are associated with youth; short, blunt tines and swept-back antlers are associated with age. A fat belly will often mean an old beast – as its teeth begin to wear, a deer will find digestion and conversion of cellulose increasingly difficult, and a starving deer will often die with a full belly rather than an empty one.

Having established how many you are going to shoot, how do you decide whether a buck that appears is to be included in the cull or not? Firstly, there must always be a conscious decision-making process, and secondly you must remember what has happened previously. Is the cull progressing according to plan, or have you made so many mistakes that you cannot afford to make another? It is no good completing your target cull in numbers, and then adding another half dozen because up to now you haven't shot any really old bucks.

Once shot, it is important to check the carcase for all the other ageing indicators. It is often said that the man who really knows the age is the one who boils the trophy. While a young middle-aged buck is an easy job, with the meat almost falling off after 25 minutes boiling, an old buck can be a fearsome job with the sinews adhering to the skull and doubling the time taken in cleaning.

The cleaning process provides an extremely useful check of age based on ossification

Older bucks keep their winter colours for longer

of the central nasal bone. The principle is that as the buck ages, the central nasal bone, in youth made up from flexible cartilage, becomes steadily more ossified along its length, the ossification starting from the inner part of the nasal system and progressing right into the extremity of the nose.

Having completed the boil, there is another very useful, but perhaps less reliable, check on age, based on examination of the pedicle. Firstly the pedicle shortens with age, and secondly there is a correlation between the thickness of pedicle against the thickness of antler at a point about 2cm above the coronet. A thin pedicle and thick antler will tend to indicate youth; a thick pedicle and a weak antler may indicate age.

Medal trophies have formed an important part of my life as a professional deer manager, and are indicative of the continuing success of deer management input. But I do not go out to shoot all the medal trophies that I see in a particular season. I assess a buck's propriety for culling by age class, and i f it has a good head, then so be it. So medal-class trophies are represented in the cull at the same percentage as they exist in the census. Medal heads often take us by surprise. Tall trophies, which at 100 metres look outstanding, often suggest youth and thus are liable to fall disappointingly below medal class. Short, thick heads often deceive in the other direction, and give a pleasant surprise.

In summary, although a full count and accurate ageing in the field is impossible, and mistakes are bound to occur, it is still possible to take a structured and deliberate cull that broadly targets the very young and the very old, while sparing the middle-aged. Best practice is difficult to achieve, but poor practice is readily avoidable. **DG**

SHOOTING THE RIGHT BUCK

Sitting down to write on one of the coldest and wettest May days I can remember, I have to wonder just how many roe kids we lose if the spring is poor. The adults are not in good condition following the endless, sunless, waterlogged winter and their fat deposits have been used up. If the flush of spring growth does not come until late, how is the doe going to make enough milk and provide sufficient nurture for twins?

Meanwhile, the buck cull has started and the question of early season selection arises. Many stalkers reported late fraying of velvet, although on my own patch I can't say that I noticed anything unusual. The old ones were clean by early April and only the young middle-aged retained velvet into early May as expected.

However, what is happening in the absence of warmth and the spring flush is that territorial activity is much suppressed. Older or heavily pearled bucks have not bothered to do a proper job of cleaning, and much dry velvet remains stuck around the coronets and backs of antlers. Furthermore, lack of territorial activity means lack of movement – the older bucks are just sitting and waiting for the weather to improve.

It can be really soul destroying to stalk in these circumstances – you see the does because they have to feed, you see the young bucks because they have an opportunity to feed without harassment by the older bucks, and you can begin to think that all the old bucks have simply deserted you!

This is bad enough when stalking for yourself on your own patch, but if you have clients out it can be devastating. This is not just because of the simple lack of success but also because of the creeping breakdown of trust that inevitably follows. I have written about this time and time again, but that doesn't make it any easier to bear.

When the temperature rises and the wind eases, things change, and you can begin to pick away at the cull. It is nevertheless my view that in general territorial activity increases exponentially as May progresses, often meaning that the most success can be enjoyed at the end of the month despite the flush of cover. But what to cull in April and early May? I'm a bit old-fashioned and prefer, when possible, not to cull an adult buck before he is in summer red coat with full colour and burnish in his antlers. But this is a personal whim, and few deer managers will have the time for such niceties.

The fact remains that, weather permitting, you will often find your oldest bucks feeding furiously and almost continuously in this early season. If you see a buck at a strange time of day, probably with very small antlers, but clean of velvet and still in full winter coat, with his face in the grass and rarely looking up – his neck

There are more indicators of age in the early season. Photo: Andy Lovel

indistinct from his body and his belly hanging fat and low – then this is almost certainly the oldest buck on the place. Once red in May, you might just mistake him at a glance for a young buck and walk straight past him. Right now the indicators of age are on your side and it is best to make use of them. There will also be territories that become un-stalkable once the cover is up, and these are bucks that are worth putting some time into now. Likewise with the poor yearlings, which I select primarily by poor body condition (taking weak antler development only slightly into account). It is extraordinary just how often the yearlings with the heaviest bodies show the weakest first-year antler growth and how pathetic little yearlings in body weight show a full six-point head. It is as well to consider carefully before lifting the rifle.

You'll often find early-season bucks feeding aggressively.
Photo: iStock

As always with roe, beware the exception to the rule. While you can be pretty sure that a buck in full winter coat in late May is older, it might only be middle aged and it might even just be sick. Similarly, although a skinny red buck in early May is almost certainly a yearling, just occasionally it might be ancient and weakening. The rule remains true that, in general, young bucks change coat first, but there are always exceptions. Similarly it is generally true that old bucks clean first, but it is also the case that a very old, non-territorial buck will frequently start to clean his antlers and then, with a lack of territorial activity, the cleaning process will stop and his antlers will become inundated with dry velvet. This might take until the end of June to clean, or even never completely clean. The better you know your patch and the better you know your bucks, the fewer mistakes you will make.

Photo: Brian Phipps

If you have the privilege of being able to wait for the rut to take the best ones among the adult buck cull, they will certainly be better trophies for it. They will look better and score better, owing to the natural oils working into the freshly cleaned and relatively porous antlers and making them darker and denser. Some deer managers believe it is right to allow those bucks the chance to pass on their genes through breeding before culling, although research done on roe suggests that the gene pool is much smaller than we thought and all of the bucks probably share the same genes anyway. Furthermore, he will already have passed on those genes during each of the previous years that he bred, and we also know that does take multiple partners during the rut. So it's an understandable sentiment, but not really supported by science.

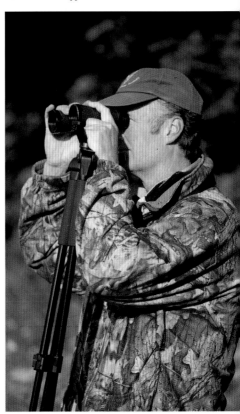

The key, as ever, is to set yourself a limit and stick to it. Long gone are the days when stalkers used to say that you could shoot a buck and it would be replaced within days. That might have been true in the 1980s when there were huge reservoirs of unstalked ground between the relatively few intensively managed areas. Today there is scarcely a farm or field without an accredited stalker and the pressure on the native roe is intense.

The impact of the additional month of March to cull does only makes things worse. We now have to completely rethink our attitude to roe management and proceed with much greater restraint than was previously necessary. **DG**

A CALL FOR COMPOSURE

Photo: Shutterstock

When spring rolls around, as a professional stalker all you ever wish for is 'ordinary' weather for the time of year. Too wet, too windy, too cold, too hot, or even weather 'on the change' – anything diverging from the norm spells bad news. And it is always the territorial males that are most reactive. Females are either about to fawn or feeding young, so they have to move. Younger bucks, in the absence of pressure from older bucks, take the opportunity to move. Only the canny territorial bucks choose sensibly to sit it out.

Day after day can pass and you begin to believe you've lost your bucks altogether. In 2012, a particularly bad year, I must have received dozens of calls from frustrated guides seeking confirmation that it wasn't just them. Well it wasn't – as far as I can see it was everyone. It was certainly the case for me.

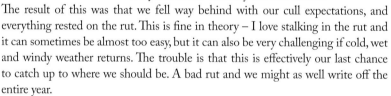

The result of this was that we fell way behind with our cull expectations, and everything rested on the rut. This is fine in theory – I love stalking in the rut and it can sometimes be almost too easy, but it can also be very challenging if cold, wet and windy weather returns. The trouble is that this is effectively our last chance to catch up to where we should be. A bad rut and we might as well write off the entire year.

The rut can be both the most exciting and the most frustrating time to stalk. From about 20 July, intense activity starts, but just when things seem unstoppable the weather can get cooler, and activity ceases just as suddenly. Your opportunities divide into two. Firstly you can simply exploit the increased activity and stalk the deer as they 'chase' around the fields, often in the open on stubble or grass fields and just as likely at 10am as at 5am. Alternatively you can wait until August and start calling in earnest.

Photo: Brian Phipps

Calling can never be considered to be unfair, as in reality its success is no more guaranteed than any other form of approach. For years I struggled, calling the occasional buck and frightening many, never feeling confident with either the noises or the technique I was using. But I was then lucky enough to meet two important influences in teaching this fascinating art. The late Prinz Heinrich Reuss taught me the technique, and Bertram Quadt (grandson of the famous author the Duke Albrecht of Bavaria), using his grandfather's original calls, taught me about the actual tone of calling. I am no expert today but I enjoy some success, with the self-confidence that at least I am doing more or less the right thing.

Of the two criteria technique and tone, technique is probably the most critical. It is no good just going into the woods and blowing – you must plan carefully for wind and select a spot where the deer can be seen approaching, but with sufficient cover to ensure the buck will be confident to make that approach in reaction to your call. Stalk into your chosen location and settle down, making sure you have a clear view behind you as well as in the direction from which you expect him to come. Then allow yourself several minutes to get accustomed to the environment.

Whichever call you use, start with a quiet and plaintive series of 'pheeps', then wait several minutes to assess any reaction. I use the Buttolo call – it is operated by hand, and as such less liable to operator error. Indeed, of all the calls this must be considered the most reliable, though not necessarily the most enjoyable to use. The noise it produces is meant to represent the squeak of a fawn or the plaintive bleat of an in-season doe.

Repeat with a louder and perhaps deeper series of calls, and again wait. At this stage I tend to use a custom-built call designed from a roe antler. This needs to be blown, or played, like any wind instrument, and it is therefore worth practising before going into the woods.

The great excitement from calling is in 'springing' a buck, when he charges in almost immediately in response to the call. I am aware that most literature suggests waiting at least an hour before moving to the next calling site, but my own preference is to try to 'spring' him and if unsuccessful move on within 15 minutes or so. No doubt I am missing many opportunities, but my feeling is that if you really wait long enough, a buck is bound to come anyway, and this does not constitute the excitement of the rut.

Success is by no means guaranteed. The weather conditions are critical – wind, cold or low pressure can significantly reduce your chances. There is also a 'critical' period, which will vary from day to day – it might be first thing in the morning on one day, but 4pm on another, and is almost certain to coincide with your chosen break for breakfast or lunch. More often than not, a doe will come first, maybe followed by a buck but maybe not. The excitement is intense, and even if the buck does come, the chance of a shot may not present itself – inevitably the buck suddenly appears behind you, or runs straight up to five metres from you, senses danger and is gone. But the experience of proximity with your quarry is exhilarating and personal.

Even if a good opportunity presents itself, you have to make a quick and accurate decision on age and suitability for culling in a way that is rare during spring stalking. And don't forget that the rut is also a great time to photograph deer, not least because increased daytime activity among the deer means the camera is not always crying out for more light.

At the peak of the rut, it really does not matter what noise you make. I remember once climbing over a stile with a client who was on the heavy side. The stile broke with a dreadful clattering and splintering noise, and as I dusted him

The bucks are active – but success is not guaranteed. Photo: Andy Lee

Dominic Griffith

down wondering whether there was any point in continuing, in charged the buck, coming to see who was challenging his territorial rights.

In fact, I often wonder whether bucks are coming to the call as much because they have sensed ingress to their territories as in reaction to the calls themselves. It is certainly the case that if you walk into a calling stand and simply wait, a buck may well come after half an hour despite the absence of calling. I suspect that in many instances the buck is lying nearby, hears something and simply remains sitting, but after half an hour his curiosity gets the better of him and he just has to come and look.

By 20 August the rut should be run and things definitely go quiet for a few weeks, although the yearlings will take the opportunity to range free from the territorial aggression of the now exhausted mature bucks. If the cull is still not complete then there should be opportunities on the stubble fields from late August through September to select the final few.

There are also nearly always a few injured mature bucks that you will find dead or dying. The most common source of injury is through bucks sparring head to head, which may result in small abrasions to the frontal bone just beneath the coronets.

The injured area will often become infected, and because the deer cannot lick the wound, it will attract fly strike. Eggs will be laid, and once the maggot has hatched, the deer will suffer a slow and obviously distressing death as the maggots eventually eat right through the flesh and skull and into the brain. Any buck in late summer that is shaking its head and appearing unwary may well have such an injury – if you see a suspected injured buck, you should put it out of its misery immediately.

I love being out in the forest in August. I love the excitement and proximity with deer. It can often provide the most important opportunity to observe, identify and cull the very oldest bucks, which have shown little of themselves all spring. But self-discipline must be shown at this time of year, and we should not exploit what can sometimes seem too easy. **DG**

DAVID BARRINGTON BARNES

David Barrington Barnes – 'the Boy Barrington' – has been shooting as man and boy for half a century. He has shot in the highlands and lowlands. He has enjoyed days spent driven shooting in a team of guns and solitary marauds on moor and marsh.

In short, he is a passionate, all-round sportsman. Since shooting his first rat at the age of eight, he has packed into life an immense schedule of shooting, stalking, and fishing. His energy and enthusiasm are remarkable, and there is not much he has not done with gun or rifle in hand.

As a writer he has become well known in the shooting press for his legal expertise and advice to fellow sportsman. However, David not only possesses a great legal mind, but an enviable ability to recall, in lucid detail, those moments in fieldsports that excite us all. This has been evident in his first book, *On The Deer Path*, where some of his experiences in stalking deer are recalled in evocative fashion, as well as his most recent work *In The Shooting Field*, recalling his varied experiences game shooting.

Today he still stalks, shoots 30 days each year and enjoys nothing more than to bring on and instruct youngsters in the shooting sports. His aim, he says, is to encourage them to pursue the pleasure that comes from country pursuits enjoyed with rifle, rod and gun.

David Barrington Barnes

GRASPING AT NETTLES

Photo: Andy Lee

I enjoy reading the stories of others who stalk roe, and also the tales of those who hunt in other countries and continents from Africa to Australia. When I have a few minutes to spare, watching a hunting video online or reading a chapter in a hunting book can be nearly as good as the real thing: it's a quick fix for the enthusiast.

Many such articles conclude with a successful cull or kill. It's understandable that a hunter wants to round off his story with a successful outcome. On reflection, I must now admit that more of my own writings end up with a beast in the larder than do my outings on the ground. I certainly don't intend to exaggerate my own success rate, so in this piece I intend to grasp the nettle of failure and unravel some of the reasons for unsuccessful stalks.

Before leaving home, it's worth going through a short checklist of essential equipment. A stalker is handicapped without a pair of boots on his feet and a pair of binoculars round his neck. It's not possible to unlock the forestry gate if you don't have the key with you. A rifle is of limited use without its bolt or the correct ammunition.

The most likely occasions for the deerstalker to leave key kit behind occur when he uses a different vehicle, travels with a friend or has a guest who arrives early and interferes with his car loading plan. If these appear to be obvious omissions, I would invite the attendees at any gathering of deerstalkers to raise their hands if they have ever left essential equipment at home. I would not expect to see many hands stay down.

On starting out for a stalk, the all-important wind direction may not readily be detected, so my car and coat pockets are full of puffer bottles to ensure I pick up the direction of the slightest breeze. That direction will often be different in the vicinity of farm buildings, woods and other obstructions. I would guess that getting the wind direction wrong is one of the most common reasons for unsuccessful stalking outings: the deer alarmed by the stalker's smell will slip off ahead of him and rarely be seen. Not infrequently, the wind will change direction during an outing.

The onset of rain during an outing cannot be avoided. Deer tolerate summer rain but chill winter rain will have them hiding under the canopy. The time, perhaps, for a stalker to find a high seat and wait for deer movement under the trees.

When there is a fresh blizzard of snow, deer will likely hide and shelter on the downwind side of a wood. A careful approach by a deerstalker in white outer clothing is quite likely to be possible, with more than one shot on the cards. Waiting for deer to move in these conditions is likely to result in failure.

Where there is intense frost at night and crisp snow on the fields, the days are likely to have Alpine blue skies and sunshine. For once, early starts are likely to fail and the top of the day may be prime time with deer, particularly fallow, throwing caution to the wind and emerging from cover for feed and sunshine. Crackling, hard frost renders moving while hunting virtually impossible because of the noise made by each footfall. Persisting in walking and stalking in these conditions is a recipe for a blank outing.

I hate stalking in fog and, if I must, I head for a high seat. If you walk and stalk in fog then deer will invariably see you before you see them because you are moving and they are still. Once, on the hill in Argyll, we followed a parcel of red deer for some miles. We never caught up with them, but continually found evidence of their recent presence.

In planning a stalk, it's sometimes difficult to avoid the disturbance caused by others. However, some dog walkers are regular in their walks on and off public footpaths. In August and September, a word with the farm foreman or tractor driver may enable the stalker to find out which fields are going to be worked over and so avoided. Anticipation of such disturbance lessens the chances of an outing being wrecked. Aerial interference with the stalk from low-flying helicopters, microlights and hot air balloons increase the chance of failure but there is little that can be done to escape them.

Moving on to defects in stalking technique, the advantages of the best-placed ambush are negated by an approach that discloses the stalker's arrival. Well prepared routes into high seats doubtless avoid a great many unproductive hours waiting for deer that departed the vicinity as soon as the stalker arrived.

In walking and stalking or still hunting, the emphasis should be on the still. Stalking too fast, or 'athletic stalking,' is a recipe for failure. When I was still practising law full time, the early part of my evening outings would see me charging over the ground in office mode and far too quickly. If I lose heart or concentration, I still find myself going too fast and, in consequence, bumping deer.

In his amusing and entertaining memoir, A Man of the Field, Frank Sheardown asserts that stopping and spying every 30 yards is the correct procedure while hunting enemy snipers or dangerous game. Sometimes in cover, under a dark canopy, I think 30 feet between each sweep of the binoculars can be far enough. Proceeding any quicker is to court failure. Fast stalking is, of course, always liable to be the cause of noisy stalking, and the combination is likely to lead to unseen deer fleeing ahead of the culprit.

Turning to the shot, some unsuccessful attempts are caused by what the stalkers concerned are likely to blame on mechanical failings. However, loose screws on rifles and optics are really the responsibility of the owner. The skilled, veteran stalker and rifleman, E. W. Holland of Colchester, once told me that he checked the tightness of the screws on his rifle and scope mounts before each stalking outing.

In the field, the reasons for unsuccessful shots encompass shooting at deer too distant, shooting in bad light, rushed shots, pulled shots and plain careless shots. If the stalker's equipment is in apple pie order, stalker error is the likely reason for a missed or wounded beast. The mantra should always be: "Accuracy is lethal." **DBB**

Stopping and spying regularly is key

A buck grassed: What it's all about

David Barrington Barnes

MEMORABLE ENCOUNTERS

Photo: Ernst Vikne

The bluebells of Bullwood have flowered many times since that late spring morning when I first encountered its great roebuck. In the half light of dawn, he stepped out of the wood in the company of a doe and follower. His rack was clean and tall, but as the light improved, the great symmetrical sweep of antler became much more apparent. However, on this first meeting it was hard to confirm how many points he had.

More impressive than his head was his body mass. He looked like a bullock in comparison with the others of his ilk. I studied him through my glasses and admired both his awesome dimensions and his masterful demeanour. I absolutely knew he was a very special roebuck. That evening I mailed the landowner's son: "Spied the best buck I have ever seen on the estate, am christening him The Bullwood Buck."

Later that same summer, when the roe rut was hot, I slipped into the back of Bullwood one sunny afternoon and concealed myself in a drift of stinging nettles. I began to call and, after a short interval, spotted the Bullwood Buck running towards me. He stopped just short and gave me the opportunity for a close-up inspection. He was a magnificent six-pointer, every bit as big in the body as I had thought on first seeing him despite the present rigours of the rut. He was obviously in the prime of his life and not for shooting.

Here I had the perfect stud buck, a veritable king among roebucks. In the hope that he would spread his genes and improve the quality of the estate's roe deer, I guarded him jealously. For several seasons, I annually called him up during the rut for close inspection. Every time I saw him I gasped – he was the absolute master of Bullwood.

Then came the sad spring when I found him desultory and displaced, now occupying a lesser territory nearby – a mere spinney with roads on every side. His back was no longer straight and his rack less regular. All this led to me calling up the owner's son and asking him to cull the Bullwood buck. He came and did what had to be done, and still has the trophy in his home. Even now, I never stalk that wood and its environs without remembering those years long gone when the Bullwood Buck was the master of its leafy dominions.

Another place and another time, I took a good friend for a summer evening stalk. "You can shoot any buck except the German's buck," I was briefed before we set off, having in mind a very fine beast I was saving for the Rhinelander. I didn't need to say anymore, thinking my experienced friend would readily recognise the reserved roebuck. During our stalk, I indicated that he should pass me, and crawl over a steep bank. As he achieved the top, I saw him tense, aim, and fire very quickly. I joined him just in time to hear him say in a chastened voice: "Oh dear; I've shot the German's buck." Swallowing the initial flush of frustration, I sighed. Oh well – it was another lesson learned.

On another occasion, this time in Argyll, a hill stalker told me of a roebuck, which had, as she said, "a funny heed". She thought this buck occupied a brackened area that was interspersed by short grass cropped by rabbits. We stalked into this bracken and took up a position overlooking the grazed turf. In response to my call, the roebuck with the funny head appeared almost at my knee before bouncing back and standing surprised long enough for me to drop him.

Looking at that trophy, as I do sometimes, I am reminded that securing a malformed roebuck trophy can be much more memorable than doing the same to a fine symmetrical roebuck. He was a young buck, perhaps only two or three years of age and so culled long before he would have been had he carried a regular head. I never ascertained the reason for the malformation, but it might have been that he became entangled in a stock fence during the growth stage. He was otherwise healthy enough.

Unusual roe are much better remembered

There is one roebuck trophy that I treasure above all others, which acquired his name after he was shot. The Lie-in-Bed Buck had lived on a grouse moor in the north-east of Scotland. That May morning, he should have been safe as winter had temporarily returned with a vengeance. Sleet and rain, driven by a strong wind, made for dreadful, hopeless stalking conditions.

My son decided to stay in bed, so I set out alone. No doubt he thought I had taken leave of my senses but I like to take every advantage I have to stalk when opportunity knocks. Heading out alone, I turned away from our comfortable abode to stalk into the teeth of the elements at a little after 3.30am.

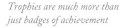

Trophies are much more than just badges of achievement

Using what shelter I could, I stalked up the main burn that winds its way through the ground. Either side of it are rough greens that give a good bite and are greatly fancied by the resident roe deer. Expecting to see nothing, and not infrequently wondering why I had gone out, I was amazed to spy a decent buck and a doe on one of these green oases. I began to worm my way close enough for a better look, and perhaps a shot, and found the conditions now favoured me as not only was any noise from my approach masked by the wind and rain but my quarry had their heads down and were feeding hard.

For the final approach, I took to the spate-filled burn, which was little hardship as I was already very wet. My heart and lung shot taken, from a convenient bump on the bank, was fit for purpose on such a rough morning, and the satisfaction I derived as I walked across the green to inspect that beast banished the wet and the cold. Now, if ever I feel like bunking off the horribly early start hour of a summer roebuck stalk, or deferring to inclement conditions, my recollection of how The Lie-in-Bed Buck met his end draws me into the woods and fields brimming with renewed anticipation. I set forth, as the saying goes, to chance a buck. **DBB**

THE TURNING SEASONS

*The rolling hills
David calls home*

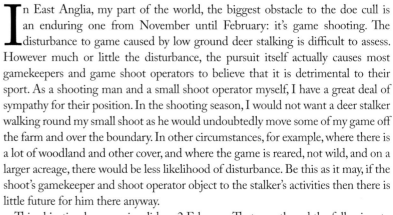

Photo: Andy Lee

In East Anglia, my part of the world, the biggest obstacle to the doe cull is an enduring one from November until February: it's game shooting. The disturbance to game caused by low ground deer stalking is difficult to assess. However much or little the disturbance, the pursuit itself actually causes most gamekeepers and game shoot operators to believe that it is detrimental to their sport. As a shooting man and a small shoot operator myself, I have a great deal of sympathy for their position. In the shooting season, I would not want a deer stalker walking round my small shoot as he would undoubtedly move some of my game off the farm and over the boundary. In other circumstances, for example, where there is a lot of woodland and other cover, and where the game is reared, not wild, and on a larger acreage, there would be less likelihood of disturbance. Be this as it may, if the shoot's gamekeeper and shoot operator object to the stalker's activities then there is little future for him there anyway.

This objection becomes invalid on 2 February. That month and the following, to a lesser extent, oblige the conscientious deer manager to go hard out at the does. I remember one February, the prevailing wind was unusually from the north and north-west for outing after outing. Going out and staying out in these conditions required a combination of gritty determination and multiple layers of clothing.

As is usual, roe deer were hard to locate in the first half of the month. Then they were more often seen out feeding on drilled winter wheat fields, even when the wind's blow was making things really 'raftery', as they say in Suffolk. No doubt I could be heard muttering such words as "grim" and "chore" more often than I should have, but the stalking was hard.

In retrospect, not all my outings were without amusement. Towards the end of an afternoon foray on 25 February, in near freezing temperatures, I spied three roe deer feeding on drilled wheat within easy range of the overgrown brook at the bottom of a sloping field. I circled round, dropped down the brook's steep banks and was able to progress downstream without difficulty for a few yards.

I then came to a stretch of concrete gabions, the downstream one of which had been moved and twisted by floodwater. It appeared I was going to get wet feet. Always game, I took a step and slipped into a hole in the riverbed that was waist deep. Well soaked, I continued my stalk and had the satisfaction of grassing the mature doe of the group.

On 28 February, as a guest rifle on a friend's ground, I carried my portable high seat the best part of half a mile in a light breeze that was on my left cheek. I set up the high seat overlooking the woodland edge, confident of a shot and pleased with my plan. Then the north wind got up and increased throughout the evening until it was blowing a bitter gale. Nothing presented for a shot (even though I'd counted 18 roe there the previous evening), though if a doe had done so I doubt

I could have hit a barn door, let alone a deer, as I was shaking and shivering with cold.

If there was one incentive to keep going at this back-end doe culling, it was, as it always is, the prospect of prime roebuck stalking in April and May. In April there was, of course, the inevitability of some overnight frosts and heavy showers, but the sting had gone out of the weather and a frosty start would likely be followed by a sunny morning. The ubiquitous muntjac and the occasional fallow pricket or sorrel might also be moving and offer an unexpected bonus cull shot.

In April the yearling bucks were being thrashed and thrown out by their fathers and uncles and the cycle of the roe deer year. Then the struggle for survival took on a fresh, fine strength and there was, to borrow Rudyard Kipling's phrase, "a spring running". By May the mature bucks and does are, or appear to be, paired. The briskness of the spring mornings is replaced by the benign warmth of early summer, with ever-lengthening days and briefer nights – a roe stalker's heavenly dream.

And then this leafy month of June screens the roe deer from view and tilts the balance of the pursuit in the deer's favour. The seeing and the stalking have all too soon been replaced by bumping and boring, when the most likely part of a buck to be seen is its white backside as it runs away.

Stalking is exhilarating whether you're on the hill...

June, then, is not a low ground stalker's month. For stay-at-home deer stalkers it's time to take a break, catch up on lost sleep, go fishing and prepare for more stalking in the rut. Another option is to head north and hunt on the hill. Up there, the summer arrives later, and the bucks are slower to come clean. The roe deer stalker can extend his prime time stalking by a month, and enjoy the exquisite pleasure of sporting stalking for hill bucks. There really is no better sport in the world than this and, if you have not experienced it, I urge you to go now while you still can.

Stalking hill roe puts more physical demands on the deer stalker than low ground stalking, but no more than a person of average fitness can handle. The fast-coming, early morning light reveals the contoured moor, while the thin, fresh air attenuates the haunting songs of hill birds. With luck, on some rough green a fine roebuck may be seen.

...or grassing a buck on the low ground

Seeing a buck is one thing, stalking it is another. Hill bucks are sharp. They have and use the advantage of view, so a lot of careful crawling may be required to get within range. Their hearing is spectacular, and the rasp of a boot on burnt heather stalks will have them running miles away. The hill birds are their friends – their alarm calls will also cause a buck to flee.

This is challenging deer stalking, providing the stalker with countless happy hours on the hill. Back home, the lightweight, elegant hill roebuck trophies are as handsome as any you will see. Souvenirs of your successes, they still cannot erase the many failures when you were bested by a buck. **DBB**

David Barrington Barnes

RUTTING REFLECTIONS

Be ready for bucks to lose their natural wariness

A young buck feeling his way before the rut proper.
Photo: Andy Lee

Whenever deer stalkers gather in advance of the rut, they dwell with obvious anticipation on what the coming rut will entail. Weather often stalls or curtails rutting activity, and there are countless other factors to consider. When you watch a roe rut in full swing, you soon realise what a powerful urge it is that gets the roebucks and does running in rings. It is those compelling instincts that cause roe in the rut to throw their innate natural caution to the wind and show themselves in ways they rarely do during the rest of the year.

The first buck I ever called and shot was in a wood, with far too much, and too tall, ground cover for calling. Taking up a position in an unkempt box-bush, I saw my calling rewarded by the appearance of a buck even more naïve than I was. I dropped him at 10 yards, threading a shot through the nettle stalks. A rut later, I called another in as close, which offered a neck shot for my son off the sticks.

That was, I recall, in a hot, active, super-charged rut packed with calling opportunities. On another morning, I installed my son in a high seat whose leaning tree was in a belt adjoining a wood. I took station on the side of the tree and seat furthest away from the wood. I made sure my son could see me, which was prudent as the buck came from my side of the tree. The perplexed roebuck worked all round my position, and it was some minutes before he moved sufficiently and stood long enough for a shot.

During another rut, I needed to cull a young buck that was causing considerable and very visible fray damage to coppice regrowth in a square, five-acre plantation. On two sides of this were arable fields outside my area, which made the plantation a difficult one to stalk. My early morning visits that spring had been unsuccessful. Meanwhile the fray damage was ongoing, and with this in mind I slithered into one corner of the plantation in the full heat of an early August afternoon.

The coppice was, again, far too dense but I began to call and in no time at all spotted the head of a roebuck having a look through the branches and leaves. I squeezed off a shot only to find to my annoyance that I had shot a mature buck.

As I started the gralloch, I became aware of a stand of hazel shaking quite violently a mere 30 yards away. I thought it was the wind until I remembered it was a still afternoon. Grabbing my rifle, I gave a couple of squeaks in response to which the young buck – my intended, original target – rushed forward and presented himself nicely for a shot.

Once in Argyll, while calling from bracken, I had a young buck race up to my knee, which prompted the comment from the observer with me that she thought I was intending to stick it with my knife.

The common thread of all these tales from the rut is that roebucks lose their natural wariness at this time. The buck who responds to the call and comes within 10 or 20 yards of the deer stalker, as on occasion they will, has his brains between his hot haunches, and really has no sense of self-preservation at all. For every individual deer stalker this raises the legitimate question as to whether buck stalking in the rut provides a worthwhile quarry at all and, if so, the subsidiary question of how we carry on in such a way that we continue to respect roe deer as a quarry while stalking during their rut.

My answer to the first question is that roebuck stalking in the rut enables me to cull surplus bucks that I never or rarely see at any other time of the season. It enables me to shoot selectively if I want or need to do so. It's a great time to take out guests, perhaps to introduce them to the sport. Finally, it's a fun time to be out on my ground.

As to the respect question, I impose some guidelines on myself and try to stick to them: not to overcall, not to hammer the same ground, not to shoot any buck primarily for its smart headgear and not to shoot any buck facing me.

Overcalling undoubtedly upsets the local roe does that often hear and respond to the call. As they will usually have dependent fawns, this can cause disturbance that should be avoided. I have seen confused does after calling. Overshooting an area during the rut has a similar detrimental impact.

The headgear point is simple. A good buck with a good head in the prime of life is the local stud. It makes sense to spare him until he goes back.

The last point, the avoidance of head-on shots, is particular to bucks called in the rut. The reason I eschew this shot is because of the frightful carcase damage that will likely be caused by a raking shot into a facing beast.

I have seen, and I am ashamed to say inflicted, some shocking examples of this. It happens because the buck so often appears at close range and the deer stalker, likely standing on the ground with sticks, has a 'now or never' moment. He does not have the luxury of knowing he can almost certainly wait until the buck turns broadside, as he does in the other months of the buck season.

No doubt some deer stalkers will consider me squeamish and other deer shooters fastidious. I don't care at all, as these are the standards that I try to apply while stalking roe bucks in the rut, although sometimes I succumb to temptation and breach them. Each to his own, I guess. DBB

Rutting activity can be magical to behold

It makes sense to spare the best bucks

David Barrington Barnes

SOMETHING OF THE NIGHT

April: A time of sunshine, fly fishing and roebuck stalking

Photo: Andy Lee

S hooting roe as darkness falls – can it ever be acceptable, or licensed? There is no doubt that the crepuscular tendencies of these beasts now come second to their nocturnal proclivities. No doubt that the harder pressed deer are by stalkers, the more nocturnal and cautious they become – so much so that an old lead doe may rarely expose herself and her followers to risk during the hours of daylight.

In the doe cull, the one hour before sunrise and the one hour after sunset shooting time that the law allows seem the times most likely to provide the key opportunities for a shot. The situation requires keen eyesight and the aid of a high-quality illuminated reticle scope. This is not to enable the stalker to shoot after 'lights out', but to perform effectively and shoot accurately, often on the edge of cover as the last light slips away and is replaced by darkness.

The circumstances are invariably worrying for the responsible deer stalker as the stricken beast, having just emerged from woodland cover, will most likely try to return to it in its death flight. By the time the stalker has got down from a high seat and followed up, what little light there was outside the wood will be even less under the canopy. A good torch and a dog can save the situation and it's remarkable how a blood trail can be followed in near darkness. While some stalkers duck evening outings because the light is running against them, those with a serious fallow cull have to get out, and can console themselves that at least they are not being required to shoot at night.

Should you think that in England just 'bad boy gamekeepers' and poachers shoot deer at night, you should think again. In late 2012, I enquired of Natural England as to the number of night licences it had issued. I was informed that for the year beginning 1 January 2012 eight licences had been issued, three for the purpose of air safety with a combined total of 15 animals, four for the purpose of preserving public health and safety with a combined licensed total of 260 animals, and one for preventing serious damage with a licensed total of 20 animals.

In response to this, I requested information as to the land parcels or estates involved in night shooting, but Natural England declined this request owing to the constraints of the Data Protection Act. However, they told me the air safety-related cull licences were in Gloucestershire, the health and safety related licences in Greater London, and that the serious damage-related licence was in Hertfordshire. By email dated 9 January 2013, Natural England also informed me that currently 18 applications are under consideration. Six relate to night shooting, and 12 to night shooting during the close season. I wondered if any of these were being made by traditional estates.

I recall raising the question of night shooting several years ago and being given the impression that although night shooting licences could technically be granted, in practice they would not be. But clearly, they are.

I have three problems with night shooting deer. The first is concern for the welfare of the deer. Some years ago, a farm I stalked was lamped for foxes by a rogue who shot the deer. I found two deer carcases that can only have been 'lost', and observed that the deer that survived on the land – which were very few – were absolutely terrified.

Secondly, deer (particularly fallow, sika and red, but also roe) stand much taller than a fox, and there is a distinct public safety issue if deer are being shot at night from, for example, a quad bike or four-wheel-drive vehicle. The bullet will be travelling at a much flatter trajectory than if fired at a fox. If you countered this concern by saying that the public will not be about at night, I would say that the public may now be found anywhere at any time, and that one or two unfortunate accidents already confirm this.

I am concerned by the apparent proliferation of licences and applications. I would like to know what the Deer Initiative and Forestry Commission have to say on the subject. Both these organisations have yet to convince me that they mean what they say when talking about balanced populations of deer.

As I have said before, our deer are a national treasure that must not be destroyed. Other 'partners' of the Deer Initiative such as BASC and the BDS may perhaps care to consider the consistency of their objectives with these 'partnerships'. Just now there seems to be a great deal of deer-phobia around and, ironically, it's for the sporting rifle shooters and those who provide such sport to protect our deer and ensure they do not once again become the persecuted animals they were before the passing of the 1963 Deer Act. There is no inconsistency in this – as Oscar Wilde wrote, "All men kill the thing they love".

Enough said. When April arrives, a deer stalker's thoughts turn to roebuck. It's time to be setting the alarm clock early and heading out in the first grey light of the spring morning. It's a month for prowling the woodland edge and the hedgerows, for spotting deer fray signs on the young whips and their slots in the soft earth of banks and burns. It's a month whose mornings give the stalker the chance to observe the bucks nibbling the tender hawthorn shoots, as they have done since their time began. A master buck cleaning up the perimeters of his kingdom, a battered, bruised, just expelled yearling, a doe getting heavy with young – these are the fine rewards for walking and stalking in the spring of the year, when all the birds sing on the April bough.

And if a buck is grassed, how much more satisfactory to take it like this than in darkness, at a time and in a way that has something of the night about it. **DBB**

Twilight hours in a field are lighter than in thick woodland

Shooting in the morning or before darkness falls maximise the chance of a clean kill and effective recovery

MARK BRACKSTONE

Mark Brackstone has made his living with the rifle at varying times in his life. He is a roe expert of long standing, and well respected in the British stalking community. He lives in Wiltshire, right in the heart of quality roe trophy country, and manages a massive area of farms and estates. Additionally Mark is a passionate big game hunter and has followed the call of Nimrod around the world, taking game species from Africa, Asia, Europe and the Americas. But it is the pursuit of the roe deer on which he has expended most of his hunting energy.

A successful sporting writer, Mark's articles have always been well received in the fieldsports press. His thirst for knowledge knows no bounds, he is never afraid to question the accepted theory on roe deer's natural history, and his thought-provoking articles are based on practical sense from observations made in the field. The modern use of trail cameras has since proved much of Mark's theory on a percentage of big bucks being wandering nomads.

As a roe caller Mark is one of the best in the business. He uses a variety of calls to suit the situation. He has guided many of Europe's leading aristocrats and captains of industry on to some quality bucks throughout the years. It is a testament to his knowledge and skill that he is known throughout Europe as the best of British roe men.

CULL PLANNING

Over the years my views on which bucks to cull have changed dramatically. Initially, like most young and inexperienced stalkers, I read numerous books and took the advice and principles portrayed by many respected and experienced stalkers. On the whole, the methods and advice given in the books worked well. I was mentored by a lovely old boy called Clive Wordley, who also set great store by what the experts had laid down.

About 25 years ago, Clive headed north to Scotland to retire, and I took over most of his ground, adding it to areas of my own. This gave me two estates and half a dozen farms, totalling around 6,000 acres – certainly enough ground to manage the deer effectively and see the results of my management plan.

Our doe cull largely comprised a count with the aim of culling a third of the population. We have many twins and some triplets in our area, so we try to cull does with a single youngster, taking the pair out if possible. If we were short on our doe cull, we would then target the poorer youngsters from the does with twins or triplets, the only problem being that at this stage – usually February – time was running short.

With regard to our bucks, up until about 15 years ago, our management cull comprised of any yearling buck with antlers shorter than his ears. Occasionally, we also culled two-year-olds with short, spindly antlers, but this was quite unusual. It took me a few years (not being the sharpest knife in the drawer) to realise that almost without exception our two-year-olds were taller than their ears. In hindsight, despite our best efforts on the yearling cull, quite a few that were shorter than the ear slipped through the net and became two-year-olds.

The rest of the cull was middle-aged bucks that had poorer antlers or were lacking in the body department. We then took out a few trophy bucks ourselves, which we considered past their best – we would often invite a friend to shoot these. My own roebuck collection comprises of bucks taken before I started taking paying guests, or swapping them with a stalker or hunter who had access to another species that I wanted to hunt. This has worked well and enabled me to experience different hunts.

To date our doe management has remained unaltered, and we aim to be pretty much done by the end of February despite the season change a few years ago. I have strong feelings on that front, but we won't go into that in this article. The big change for us in management practice is where our bucks are concerned.

This was as a result of two extraordinary coincidences. We had a yearling buck with a sort of inverted left ear. I first saw him as a kid, and for many months thought that he had a white ear. I got to know this buck as he was so recognisable and lived close to my house. As a yearling he was a very poor-looking four-pointer, but as he was so distinctive I left him despite the fact that his antlers fell well below the level of our cull principle. The following season we had a kid with a white head and neck

Culling the poorer youngsters might not always be the best option.
Photo: Andy Lee

Thorough approach:
Mark's 2007 cull plan

Photo: Andy Lee

in a completely different area. This unusual buck was off our boundary most of the time and I agreed with a neighbouring keeper that we would leave him to get old as we could both recognise him.

The yearling with the inverted ear, nicknamed Whitie, produced an impressive second head despite the poor yearling antlers. His third head must have been just short of a bronze quality head; his fourth was probably silver quality. Then he mysteriously vanished. We had tyre marks over the wheat fields in his area and we surmised that he had been poached.

The buck with the white head likewise produced three heads, each exceeding normal expectations. He died as a result of an RTA (road traffic accident), and a nearby landowner delivered me his partly decomposed head. I cleaned the head and got it measured; it achieved a high silver at 124 CIC points at four years of age. It is the only buck on my wall that I didn't shoot.

Our stalking is in the heart of Wiltshire, which is known for consistently producing high-quality trophy bucks. In my mind I had proven beyond doubt that a large portion of our bucks, if allowed to get old, could produce high-quality trophies despite many of them having an inferior first head.

By the time we changed our culling policy, we had increased our management area to some 30,000 acres of mixed stalking. This holding has remained pretty much unaltered, although we have gained and lost odd bits of ground on occasion.

What has changed considerably is our buck cull percentage. It is now made of 80 per cent old trophy bucks, with the remaining 20 per cent being animals that are just poor regardless of antler quality. Over the same acreage we have consistently taken three times the number of trophy bucks that we did previously. That said, roe numbers right across our area have fallen over the last few years, but that is the subject of discussion for another day.

Possibly because of the trace elements, minerals and no doubt the gene pool, our area is unique with regards to consistently producing quality heads. That said, we have certainly turned the long-accepted principles of roe buck management on their head (excuse the pun).

Most of our spotting for shootable bucks is carried out during January and February. My colleague Robert and I carry a notepad. Whenever we see what we consider to be an old and/or shootable buck, we make a note of its location, the date and as accurate a description as possible. When we reach March or early April, we compile a shortlist – usually 10 to 15 of the big bucks we know of and think we may cull with our spring clients. We try to get a better look at each buck and note if and when it is clean of velvet, and make our final assessments. They always look massive in velvet, making you think you're going to have a number of golds, but when they become clean they always seem to shrink.

By the time the spring clients arrive in mid-April, we have a list of bucks with a description and location. For our own interest and for fun, Rob and I put a percentage chance against each buck. This relates to the chance we think the client has of culling that particular beast – not based on marksmanship but on location, behaviour and other variables.

We do the same for the summer hunt, recceing from June until mid-July to produce another list of new bucks found or moved in. Any bucks not culled on the spring list are automatically added to the summer sheet if still present. I'll take some examples from the 2007 list to show how we do things:

Spring buck No. 1 – client missed. We recorded it as a miss because no reaction was noted, and no blood or pins were found. However, I later wondered if it was in fact hit or got a big fright, as this buck was never seen again.

Spring No. 2 – a new buck appeared after the spring buck cull – see summer buck number two.

Spring buck 6 did not get culled at that time and was re-entered on the summer sheet as buck 3; he was successfully culled in the rut.

Spring No. 8 – this buck was not taken in the spring but went onto the summer cull sheet as buck No.6 and was culled in the rut.

These are just a few examples and they do make interesting reading. We reckon that over the last 10 years, 65 per cent of the spring bucks we take are on our list, the other 35 per cent made of suitable bucks we just happen upon. In the rut we sometimes wonder why we bother to recce as only 40 per cent of the bucks we take are on our sheet – 60 per cent are strange bucks to us that just turn up.

Whether our cull information is of interest to others in similar areas I can't comment, but what I can say is that we have devised a method that works very well for us, and on the rare occasions we can't find a buck, at least the client has something to read and still strive for.

Producing a list of available bucks to the client looks professional and instantly puts them at ease. It is proof that the homework has been done. Recceing and assessment is the real hard work – if this has been done diligently, you have gone as far as possible to create your own good luck. **MB**

A good example of a malformed head

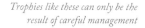

Trophies like these can only be the result of careful management

Mark Brackstone

TERRITORIAL OR TRAVELLER?

In my 30 years as a semi-professional stalker I have culled a large quantity of roe deer. Like many stalkers I spend a lot of time out recceing for bucks for my clients, who all want a gold medal roe buck of course. I am fortunate that my wife, Helen, can aid me in this department as she spends a lot of her day on horseback and, complete with binoculars and a telescope, locates a lot of bucks for me.

In my early days as a stalker I read every book about stalking I could get my hands on, especially about roe. I soaked up this information and later learned many tips first-hand from my mentor, the late Clive Wordley from Wiltshire, and have been a deer manager ever since. Over the years I've formed an opinion I've not yet seen in any books. I truly believe that a high percentage of the really big bucks don't hold a territory in the same way as many a run-of-the-mill buck commonly does.

I think that many of these impressive bucks are almost transient, simply moving from one territory to the next, and it is my belief that this happens throughout the summer and not just in the spring when roe bucks are sorting out and defending territories.

Maybe it's just my ground, which covers a big part of Wiltshire, but if you are an experienced deer manager, ask yourself how many times you have seen a huge buck once, or maybe a couple of times in an area, but then never again. I would suggest that this is a common occurrence.

I can only put forward my own experiences but I have at least enough evidence of my own to convince myself of the accuracy of this theory.

The trophy buck I'm pictured with overleaf came from a walled estate of 2,000 acres. It's difficult for the resident deer to leave or for others to enter this estate but it's not impossible, as events later proved. However, being almost walled-in makes particular bucks easier to locate, enabling one to keep tabs on them pretty well. I first saw this buck in early April. I marked him as a client buck and moved a high seat into his location. In the middle of April he was nowhere to be found, until he turned up in another area when I was recceing a mile or so away. I put this down to another one-off sighting of a transient buck. In June I once again caught up with the same buck a few miles further away from the walled estate. In the rut, by chance, I bumped in to him in a completely different area where my client shot him.

The reed call: Difficult to master but worth the effort

I believe that this buck came into the estate through one of the holes in the wall and used the whole estate as his territory, displacing the bucks that were usually territorial there. He must also have passed through many other mature bucks' territory.

In my time as a professional deer manager I have probably seen eight or 10 exceptional bucks of immense proportions, only to never see them again. Is this just coincidence or are they exercising their right to roam in view of their impressive headgear, large bodies and their obvious dominance over lesser rivals? I personally believe that this last assumption is very much the case.

The Buttolo: Excellent for long-range calling

I stalk over some large tracts of down land, of many thousands of acres, and the topography means you get to know individual bucks and their particular territories very well. I saw the malformed buck pictured here in one

location in the middle of April. He spent a week there with a smaller buck and three does. By early May he had moved about two miles through two other bucks' territories which were known to me, and had displaced another buck. But by late May he had moved another two and a half miles away and again displaced the resident buck. Unfortunately for him this is where he met his Waterloo.

Consider the two bucks above and then look over the CIC gold medal heads recorded annually in the sporting press, particularly

referring to those bucks that have been found dead, presumably as a result of road casualties. I have noticed over the years that many of the deer that I have found killed by road traffic accidents have been very large bucks indeed. Are they knocked down when chasing inferior rival bucks or are they simply transient and more likely to meet their fate on the tarmac due to their nomadic lifestyle?

During the rut, we all know that a doe can draw or even bring a buck back into her area but when you know your own area well and know all of the resident bucks, you begin to wonder whether she really travels miles to find that impressive big buck that appeared from nowhere. I rather think that he would be on the move anyway and just arrives in the vicinity having travelled many miles, instead of being enticed in by the female.

When you consider my experiences and think about the really big bucks that you have seen once only – or twice at most – and then vanished, maybe you will agree that this theory holds some water. **MB**

Buck master: Mark with a trophy buck

BRONZE BUCK BONANZA

I found myself indebted to *Sporting Rifle*'s editor, Peter Carr, as he had kindly recommended me to a German gentleman who had come to the UK and stalked with me on a number of occasions over the last few years. Pete had never asked for any commission, and when I mentioned this to him his reply was that he could not take anything from me, but he would love to join me for a good roebuck.

We agreed some dates and the scene was set. To say that I was a little nervous guiding someone who also had a wealth of experience in the stalking game was an understatement.

The clients had gone a few days earlier and I still knew of a good old buck that would possibly be a bronze and should fit the bill perfectly. Peter would be with me for an evening stalk as well as a stalk the next day, morning and evening.

On the way to an area where a big buck lived we chewed the fat and discussed our various adventures around the world. The pressure was on me to produce something, but this had to be pretty minimal compared to what Peter must have been experiencing.

We crept into position to watch the face of the wood. We continued to talk in whispers as the light started to fade. A young buck came out and trotted down the field but there was still no sign of the mature buck. I whispered that I would creep around the corner and check to see if he was out on the back of the wood.

I checked out the other side but all was quiet. As I returned I scanned the field and there was the old boy coming out of the wood. I looked at Peter who was still watching the yearling, and slowly approached him. "He's out, Pete," I hissed, "By the wood."

With that the buck ran down towards the yearling. The light was receding fast as we were in the shadow of a big bank with a wood above. I watched as the yearling neatly out-manoeuvred the resident buck, and whispered, "Take him when you're ready, Pete." He had his .243 Heym on the sticks and moved the safety forward. The bucks were now 130 or so yards from us and 30 yards apart.

I was looking at the bucks through a pair of 10x50 binos and could see the big buck well. Peter had tracked it with the rifle but had glanced my way as the bucks had skirted around one another. He was sitting using my sticks and I was half standing behind him. I glanced down and could immediately see that he had the rifle trained on the youngster. We had earlier had a fair bit of banter about a mutual acquaintance who'd had this kind of bad luck, and I'd even sowed the seeds of doubt in Peter's head when I jokingly said: "Imagine if you miss in front of me."

My knee-jerk reaction was to quickly advise Peter that it was the wrong buck, but it was at this moment that the small trident-holding devil popped up on my shoulder. I thought to myself: "It's only a poorish yearling – and how much piss-taking at Peter's expense is this going to be worth over the years?"

Mark and Pete got on to some quality bucks after passing over a youngster

Photo: Andy Lee

I suppressed a chuckle and got a grip. "It's too dark, Pete," I said. "Let's come back in the morning." The look of disbelief and disappointment on Pete's face was a picture. He said, "I could have taken him no problem."

With that I passed him my binos. He looked at the buck he thought was the big one, then swiftly swung them a few degrees to the other, let out a huge sigh and grinned at me. He looked accusingly at me with a wry grin and said, "You bugger, you considered letting me do that, didn't you?" I burst out laughing, and still kick myself to this day for letting the esteemed editor off the hook. Next time he won't be so lucky.

We returned at first light and I watched Peter make a 100-yard crawl before taking that same old buck with a textbook heart shot. The buck was a superb old trophy and had probably gone back slightly. I reckoned he would be around a bronze as long as he had a fair density of antler, which most of our bucks tend to do.

After handshakes and a clap on the back, we loaded up and headed for a different area to look for a buck I really didn't expect to see – but I was not worried as I had already fulfilled my offer of a good Wiltshire roebuck.

Sometimes you get a real red letter day. We had walked about 200 yards from the vehicle and really not even started stalking properly when Peter nudged me – a buck had appeared around the corner of the hedge no more than 50 yards away.

*It's a triple
treat for Pete*

*Consistent antler quality indicates
an effective management plan*

We froze, as did the buck. He had seen us, but was not sure what we were. Luckily, Peter had taken the rifle from his shoulder the second he spotted the deer, but I had the sticks and could not move. I recognised the buck as the one I wanted Peter to take. I gently nodded once. Now, at that moment, had I been on the rifle, I would have gently lifted it and put the crosshairs on the buck. But Peter adopted a different approach, as quick as a flash up came the rifle, the safety released and the bullet away in about one and a half seconds. The buck just collapsed in a heap as the 100-grain Nosler caught him dead centre of the chest.

I just said 'lucky' and Peter looked at me with a smirk and cocked his eyebrows; another buck in the bag and probably another bronze. Peter was delighted. "Which bit was lucky?" he asked.

"Everything! First we found him, second he stood long enough while you buggered about, and thirdly that you hit him." Peter just chuckled and took my jibe in good spirit, having two good-sized Wiltshire bucks, both potential bronzes.

It was still too early to go home so I took Peter to an area where I really didn't expect to see anything, but where we could kill a bit of time. Just before he climbed into a high seat on the edge of the wood he asked me what the buck that we were looking for was like. With tongue firmly in cheek, I said lightly: "Oh, he's a fair one. You'll know him if you see him, and I'll be back in an hour."

I walked back to my Land Rover and settled down for a snooze, leaving Peter watching the birds and other wildlife going about their business before the sun got too hot.

Only 10 minutes had passed and I was just nodding off when I heard a whack, followed a split second later by the muffled boom of the moderated rifle going off. This was unreal – what had he shot now?

When I got to the high seat, Peter was busy propping up yet another old buck for photos. You guessed it: it was a third bronze. It was a really nice one and Peter was all smiles.

On the way back to breakfast he let me off the hook for the previous evening's stalk by announcing that he had had a really great time and this was, in his career, the first time that he had shot three trophy bucks before breakfast. I told him not to expect to come back next year as he was just too darned lucky, and this was his commission off next year's hunt if his German friend re-booked.

I must say I really enjoyed our time together but I will regret not letting him shoot the yearling the night before. I bet I never get another chance to have one over on the infamous Mr Carr. I shall be kicking myself forever more. **MB**

BACK IN BLACK

A dark roebuck may not always be what it seems

Crucial moment: Robert takes the shot

When you play custodian to a roe population for many years you should, if you are spending enough time on the ground, know most of your resident bucks. Yet however diligent you are, you do sometimes get real whoppers – often transient younger bucks that have been displaced from another area – who just turn up.

Every reader who has a fair amount of experience will also know that certain patches of ground, or a particular copse, will almost always hold a good roebuck. If you remove the resident buck in the spring, by mid-summer his replacement has arrived. My guess is that these prime spots hold food, cover, shelter, and are usually quiet.

On a small farm near my home – which is mainly meadows and so devoid of copses and woodland – the roe are all hedge dwellers. Surrounding us are beef farms, so the roe frequently have to move to cattle-free areas.

Early one rut I took out an old medal head buck that I had seen many times over the last year – it had just appeared as a five-year-old. Although reluctant to do so, I also took a late hunt to help out a colleague. Three Danish guests arrived around 10 August, at which point the rut in our area is pretty much over, but I was willing to try calling and see if we got lucky.

A couple of days before the clients arrived I bumped into the farmer on whose land I'd taken the medal head buck. I told him about the buck, and that he could expect some remuneration in the next few weeks, although there were no other mature bucks on his land old enough to take out just now. He replied that a black one he'd seen looked pretty big. "A black one?" I was intrigued, and asked him to describe it to me. My initial thoughts were that he had probably seen a stray black fallow. Our nearest fallow are about eight miles away, and it would be a first for me to pick one up in this area.

I quizzed him further and asked him to describe it as accurately as he could, bearing in mind that to him a deer is a deer regardless of species – it sounded like a roe, but a black one?

His final sentence convinced me though: "Well, the last time I saw it was last Monday, and it was chasing another deer without horns round and round a clump of thistles for over an hour!" A roebuck rutting, I thought to myself, and thanked him for the info. I needed to get a look at this buck and quick: I had never seen a black one. About 12 years ago we took one with a white head and neck that now has pride of place over a Belgian Count's mantle, and I was curious by the thought of a melanistic roebuck.

The following morning my stalking partner Robert and I met at 5am and, armed with our binos and telescopes, we went in search of this alleged black roebuck. We agreed to stalk half the ground each and keep in radio contact with one another. As we parted I muttered something about eating my hat if we had a black roebuck on our patch, as I hadn't seen it before.

Robert pointed out that on a neighbouring farm two years ago there had been a pure white albino buzzard born – so these things do happen. But after about an hour I must have worked my way around 100 acres of ground, and had seen only one lone middle aged buck, a yearling chasing a young doe, and a doe with a pair of fawns skipping along behind her – no black buck.

Then my radio crackled and Robert's voice whispered: "Mark, are you there?"

"Yes, what have you seen?"

"I got him," he replied, and proceeded to explain that he was a good, mature buck, lying tight by a hedge in the early morning sun.

From what Rob could see his head was not black although his body looked to be grey. When it stood up and walked into the shade, its body then looked black. As we manage the deer on most of the farms in this area, how on earth could a nearly black buck have escaped my notice for so long?

Two days later I was guiding my Danish client. We were looking for this old black buck that had appeared from nowhere. On our very first outing we got a fleeting glimpse of it chasing a doe: there was some rutting still going on, despite the fact that we were now well into August.

As I watched the buck through my binos I thought it strange that although his body was indeed black, his head was still a normal red colour. Robert had been correct, and he was sporting a fair set of antlers.

We continued to stalk the area but to no avail. Over the next two days we paid regular visits to that spot, but the black buck had vanished. On the last morning of the hunt Robert took the guy for one final look for it. I had finished stalking with the other client and was on my way to the game larder with a nice buck when I got a call from Robert: "We got it, but you should see it."

Before he could say anything else I blurted out: "Whatever you do, don't cut its head off. My client might want a cape mount, as it's black."

But Robert simply replied: "You need to see this. It's not what you think it is."

It took me 15 minutes to reach Robert, and when I got there I was astonished. The whole of the buck's body was almost devoid of hair, and his skin was a charcoal grey colour, giving it the appearance of being black.

I examined the buck for lice, but could find none. He was in good condition: the humps and all organs seemed completely normal, although it did have a few scrapes down its body. The surface of the skin was powdery in some areas, similar to that found on humans suffering from eczema or dermatitis, and I wondered if this buck had some sort of dermatological problem or was infected by a microscopic louse.

The photos were taken and the hunter had a lovely head to take away. I intended to take the carcase for testing, but unfortunately my freezer broke down. By the time we realised, the contents were destroyed, and we have never found out the reason for the buck being bald. I am still pondering that one today. **MB**

Hair raising: A lack of hair caused the confusion

It's not every day you get to grass a buck like this one

Mark Brackstone

KEEP YOUR HEAD

You've put all that effort into finally getting that trophy of a lifetime, so now you want it to last a lifetime. So how do you properly prepare that prize head at home? Although this is not a definitive guide to the preparation of your hard-earned trophy, I have found this to be a reasonably efficient method, which produces the desired result. My instructions are for roe and muntjac, but the same applies for the larger deer – except that you will need a larger saw and boiling pot.

1. Now that you have your trophy, the first job is to skin the head carefully.

2. Years ago we used to saw the skull with a wood saw by eye, but it left lots of room for error and we had our share of mistakes. We now use a purpose-made jig and saw, which is adjustable and readily available from any of the shooting supply people who advertise in this magazine.

3. I like to see the full eye sockets and the full nose on my skulls when they are on a shield, but the jig is fully adjustable. I put the skull in the jig and set the same distance each side. I set mine from the ear hole to the end of the nose. (For muntjac, cut from the ear holes to about 0.5in back from the tusks. This will keep the tusk sockets intact, and allows you to glue them back in before mounting the skull on your shield.)

Every skull sits differently in the jig so you need to adjust it for each. It is helpful to have an assistant at this stage; one holds the jig and one cuts with the saw. When you are almost through, make sure you support the section you are cutting off. If it falls away, you will snap the end of the nose bones.

Note that a warm, recently shot skull is infinitely easier to saw than one that is a few days old or has been frozen and thawed out. Not being a scientist, I don't know the reason, but some transformation must occur that changes the bone composition.

4. Now comes the smelly bit. You must Submerge the skull, although preferably not the antlers, in a pot of boiling water. In the past, we used to use an old boil-type washing machine – just like your granny had. We have since invested in a Burco water boiler, which is ideal.

We then add some washing-up liquid. The purpose of this is to disperse the grease that is produced in the process, and makes it easier to remove any scum from the antlers when it's finished.

The next thing to do is to boil the skull for around 20 minutes. The skulls of old bucks probably need an extra 10 or so minutes, whereas a young buck (roe or muntjac) requires about five minutes fewer than the original time. It is important to be very careful with this step, as if you overcook a young skull it can easily fall apart. Then you will need to be good with a jig saw and have some superglue to hand!

5. Once boiled, the ideal method is to use a power washer to blast all of the flesh, gristle and brains from the skull. We have an old vice set on a sleeper, but you can easily put your welly on one antler and do it like that. A set of wet gear is ideal, as you can get covered in various bits of waste matter if you're not careful.

Do not power wash the antlers themselves, as you will remove all of their natural colours. If the antlers are covered in scum just hold them under the tap and give them a light scrub with a washing-up brush.

Take care with the end of the nose as it is easy to shatter it with a powerful jet wash and, believe me, it takes some time to find the small bits of nose bone when they fly off at Mach four in a shower of spray!

You may find that you need to do a bit of scraping with a knife to finish the job, and a long-nosed pair of pliers is useful to remove the brain membrane.

If there's still a lot of meat and gristle remaining after the power wash, loosen it up a bit with a knife and pop it back in the boiler for another five minutes then try again.

6. Your skull is now a grey-brown patchy colour. To make it white, you will need hydrogen peroxide, which you can buy from any chemist. Better still, if you know a hairdresser they should be able to get a discount through the trade (purchase the liquid, not the cream, if possible). Use a solution of as strong a percentage as you can buy.

Take care not to get any onto the antlers or your skin – peroxide burns and turns the skin white. Allow your skull to dry partially and scrub off any scum from the antlers. Pour the peroxide solution into a Tupperware or similar dish and use a tablespoon to ladle the solution carefully onto and into the skull.

If you do accidentally get the solution on the antlers, wash it off immediately. Many years ago I accidentally got a good amount on the palm of a fallow antler, and the next morning there was a hole almost the size of a 50p piece through it.

Leave the solution on the skull for 20-30 minutes and then wash it off carefully with cold water.

7. Prop your skull up and leave it to dry completely. The skull will go white as it dries and, once dry, it is ready to fix to a shield.

8. If your head had velvet on the antlers or was still in velvet early on in the season, the antlers will now be white. You can colour them with potassium permanganate, which you can buy in the form of a small pot of crystals from the chemist.

Mix a quarter-teaspoon of crystals with two teaspoons of warm water and mix well (the resulting liquid will be mauve). Using a small paintbrush you can then colour the antlers. Within minutes they will start going brown (as will anything else you get the mixture on, so be warned, as wives and partners take a dim view of a multi-coloured sink and the dye is not easily removed).

It's a good idea to practise on a scrap antler first as you can dip the brush in clear water and dilute the mix as you get close to the antler's correct tones, which feather out to an almost white colour on the tips.

If you intend to have the head trophy measured for a medal, don't stain it first, as the measurer will almost certainly be experienced enough to recognise that it's been coloured. If coloured well, however, it looks fine afterwards when on the wall.

ROE RUT SPECTACULAR

Photo: iStock

Jan put his .243 onto the cross sticks and aimed at the massive buck that was courting a doe. He breathed deeply, getting his nerves under control, then applied pressure to the trigger. The crack from his rifle rang out; the buck spun around, trying to locate the source of the disturbance, and then ran. My heart missed three beats. I was dismayed – after all this, he had missed it.

But it started a long time before that…

In the build-up to the rut, we spent many hours going on recce for old trophy bucks. We knew of about 15, but in June I had seen an absolute monster but from a considerable distance. The antlers looked very thick, possibly in a weird configuration, but he vanished before I could get my Grey & Co draw scope on him for a clearer image.

I returned to the area three or four times during July in an attempt to locate and evaluate his headgear, but never got a further glimpse of him. I put it down to my 'transient buck theory', and assumed he had been on walkabout and had since moved on to pastures new.

Three days before Jan and his friend arrived, I decided to visit the area again. Feeling lazy, I opted to crawl around the headlands on the quad bike; every now and then I would stand on the rear rack and glass areas or look over hedges from my elevated position.

I went around each field, carefully spying for half-hidden roe heads in the cereal crops. I saw quite a few bucks, does and kids but nothing to really excite me.

I ended up travelling along the head of a bean field. Conscious that at three to four feet high, the beans would completely hide any deer, I failed to give the crop much attention. I was halfway along one side of the 40-acre field, standing on the footrests to look over the hedge, when a movement in the beans about 50 yards away caught my attention. A large area had been missed by the drill when planting the beans, or maybe pigeons had damaged it; in any case there was about half an acre where the crop was sparse and weeds had grown to a couple of feet.

Stopping the quad and raising the binoculars, I spied a buck's ears and a pair of thick black antlers with several points. I carefully stood up on the quad seat and focused intently on the buck. My pulse raced and adrenalin flowed through my veins. This was a spectacular buck, carrying a normal but heavily pearled thick antler on the left and a small forest of tines on his right antler. The abnormal antler really was magnificent – to my excited mind it was the thickness of a cake tin at the base. As flies were pestering the buck, he would not keep still long enough for me to count the tines, but I had no doubt this was a very special trophy buck.

Jan arrived with his friend; I told him that we had some good old bucks for him to try for, and would he like to try for a thick, non-typical buck? He asked me

A vehicular recce was first up

what it looked like; I found a biro and paper and did a quick, poor-quality sketch for him. Jan's response was: "Yes, yes, I must have this buck."

The following day I took Jan to the vicinity where I had seen the trophy buck. First we stalked the area, and later I drove around the bean field in my Land Rover, stopping at various spots where I could stand on the bull bar and look into the beans. After two hours of searching to no avail, we left the area and went to look for another animal, which luckily we found and harvested.

Over the next two days, events pretty much stayed the same, except that on a couple of occasions we saw a two-year-old buck with a doe in the area where I had originally seen the malformed buck. Both Jan and I knew that this was not a good sign – it looked like the big buck had probably moved on. On the third evening we went around the bean field and saw nothing – an outcome we were getting used to – and we proceeded to stalk around the adjacent wheat field. Just as our hope was all but lost, we rounded the field corner and I saw two deer not more than 80 yards away. I guessed it would be the two-year-old buck and raised my binos slowly, but I gasped as I realised it was the old boy. Once again I paused to appreciate just how good he really was.

After deploying the stalking sticks, I whispered smartly to Jan: "That's him, take him when you can." That's when he missed. In my extensive experience, once a hunter misses he is usually experiencing buck fever – and if he is, it is only going to get worse.

The buck and doe paused at about 100 yards, but due to the moderator he had thankfully still not clocked our location. Jan continued to track him with the reloaded rifle. I sternly whispered to Jan: "Do not shoot unless you are sure." The last thing I wanted was a wounded deer, especially when we were this close to an extremely thick bean crop. There was an atmosphere of intense anticipation – which was then shattered by a long crack from Jan's rifle. The buck collapsed. "Reload and cover his position," I instructed, spying the buck's still form and looking for any signs of life.

We waited like this for five minutes or so until the doe wandered off. I looked at my hands, and to my surprise they were shaking. Even I had a touch of buck fever.

We approached Jan's buck and what a superb old trophy buck it turned out to be. He had 10 points, which later weighed at 640g; were he not malformed would easily be of gold medal status on weight alone. Our perseverance had paid off. Jan was absolutely delighted and asked me to cape the buck for taxidermy. I estimated the buck to be seven years old as his teeth were well worn. The bullet had entered the boiler room a little high and shocked the spine, causing him to collapse, but he had quickly succumbed and died almost instantly.

The two-year-old we had seen also showed lots of promise, and would probably benefit from the removal of the old buck. I could not help but wonder if I might be lucky enough to find him again in the future, when he was six or seven years old and hopefully haunting the same area. **MB**

Jan eventually overcame the dreaded buck fever

It was a special roebuck to crown the stalk

CHRIS DALTON

An experienced stalking guide, Chris Dalton runs South Ayrshire Stalking and primarily operates across South Ayrshire, but he has ground across the whole of Scotland. While he has stalked a wide range of quarry, both what Scotland has to offer and further afield, it is the management of roe on which he spends most of his time.

Whether out on his own or with clients, Chris is at the coal face of deer stalking 365 days a year. His experience is unparalleled and as a result he has become a leading deer stalking writer in *Sporting Rifle* magazine. But it all started years earlier, with a full military career as a commissioned officer in the RAF specialising in security. Following retirement from the service he ran a horticultural nursery in West Yorkshire – he has always been a countryman with an interest in natural history. His sporting interest developed from airguns around the farm, through pigeons, driven game and eventually stalking.

Chris set up South Ayrshire Stalking in 2005, where he is now assisted by stalking partner Tony and wife Anne. A self-sufficient estate, South Ayrshire serves its own venison to guests and caters for everyone from experts to complete novices in an unspoilt part of Scotland. Through his stalking, guiding and writing, he's built a deserved reputation as a roe expert north of the border.

Chris Dalton

SO YOU WANT TO GO STALKING

I started stalking just as it seemed to gain momentum, and there was a real national interest in getting involved. It seemed to coincide with an increase in the distribution of deer across the country, which must have had something to do with it, but clearly there were many other factors at work. If you believe the results of surveys done by some of the sporting organisations in recent years, then demand for stalking continues to grow at quite a pace. I found from my own experience of coming from a rough and game shooting background that it was quite difficult to get into stalking unless you were fortunate enough to have family connections, land with deer present or a mate who was stalker and willing to take you out. As I had none of these, my route at that time was to do a DSC 1 and then join a syndicate. It worked, but it certainly wasn't ideal. I spent most of the first year walking round the woods, not finding deer, and on the odd occasion when I did spot one it was a white backside bouncing away into the undergrowth. I eventually started to get the hang of it by making just about every mistake I could – and you could argue that that is not a bad way to learn! Anyhow, that is primarily why one of the first packages I offered at South Ayrshire Stalking was an Introduction to Stalking (a course as popular now as it was 10 years ago).

Why I am mentioning this? Because in my career as a professional stalker, the questions I get asked the most are all about how to get into stalking, how to get

Photo:
Shutterstock

*It's vital to get tutelage
from an experienced stalker*

access to land and how to go about getting a rifle. I spend more time discussing these issues now than I ever did before, and the demand for our introductory courses continues. While I do not want to get into the policies of different police firearms departments, and I do not claim to be an expert in such matters, I deal with many of the firearms departments' processing applications for grants of FACs for deer legal rifles on a regular basis. I think I can, therefore, offer practical advice on the best way to tackle the process, making it as painless as possible.

To stalk on your own you need a rifle, and to get a rifle you need an FAC. The two main steps to achieving this are firstly to demonstrate competence in the use of the rifle and an awareness of the legal and safety aspects involved, and secondly to provide good reason for wanting the thing in the first place. Put these two elements in place and you should have no problems (I am assuming you have no criminal record of note, and I don't mean speeding points).

Let's look at training first. There are various options here, although ultimately the police will want you to have completed your Deer Stalking Certificate level 1 (DSC1). This assessment includes: a range test, a safety assessment, a visual test, two multiple-choice papers, a general paper and a large game handling paper.

*Proving your competence
with a rifle is key, of course*

Again, there are a number of ways to achieve this. On one hand, you can attend the full blown four-day course, which takes you through everything in a classroom environment and usually has around 10-14 candidates at a time. On the other, you can self prepare and simply attend the assessment.

At Garryloop we prefer to do a mix of the two, usually with a maximum of four candidates, which allows more instructor attention and a slightly more relaxed environment. Our candidates self prepare and we do a revision/training afternoon the day before the assessment. This works very well for us, and produces a high pass rate. The DSC is a recognised qualification and you will need to put the work in to pass: it is not open book, but a fair and honest assessment – despite what you may hear!

We increasingly find that folk want to do the Introduction to Stalking course either a month or two before their DSC or at the same time, thereby combining the practical elements of stalking with the more formal training and qualification aspects. It also ticks most boxes a firearms enquiry officer will be looking at before deciding on your suitability for a firearm, and certainly demonstrates your commitment. Most importantly, you get practical advice and extensive knowledge of all different aspects of stalking and the law. I would have gained a lot from such instruction in my early days, and would certainly have had some venison in the freezer a lot sooner!

Now to tackle the 'good reason' for owning your deer rifle. These days, firearms staff will want you to have permission to stalk ground on a frequent basis. Not so long ago, when it would have been acceptable to pay for the odd day. The ideal scenario is therefore to have permission to shoot on a suitable area of land with deer on it. This isn't easy to achieve for any kind of shooting, and even more difficult in the case of deer. If you can offer your services to a farmer who is having a problem with deer then you are indeed fortunate, especially as an inexperienced stalker learning your trade. Be persistent and don't be disheartened: if you don't ask you don't get! With a polite approach, you never know, you might just be in the right place at the right time. Better still, if a personal introduction through a contact or friend is possible, be sure to take advantage of it. You can also join local shoots, and offers to help the keeper or estate owner with pen building or the like can occasionally result in stalking opportunities. A more realistic option is to join a stalking syndicate; you will see quite a few of these advertised in the sporting press. Price varies massively, and be very wary: there are cowboys out there trying to make a fast buck. I would certainly ask around before parting with your money – speak to an existing member and go and have a look around first. I still hear of syndicates being advertised as five rifles when in reality there are 35 – you have been warned!

The above is given as a general guide: individual circumstances will vary and different rules may apply. I deal with firearms staff across the country on a regular basis and find them to be, in the main, a very helpful breed. None of the people that I have assisted through this process – of which there are many – have ever had cause to complain. I also find that with somewhere to use the rifle and a confirmation of booking for a DSC 1, most forces will grant an FAC so that you may use your own gun for your DSC range assessment. Good luck and get on with it: the opportunities are out there if you fancy stalking, and it's not nearly as difficult as you think! CD

Venison dinner: This is what it's all for!

Chris demonstrates the gralloch

Chris Dalton

DOS AND DON'TS OF THE DOE CULL

Photo:
Shutterstock

Photo:
Andy Lee

November, when the bucks are done and the doe cull begins, is a time I particularly enjoy. The dreaded midge has gone, the cover is down and we get those lovely frosty mornings with clear blue skies. You can sit and relax over a meal and a dram or two in the evening and still have a decent night's sleep and lie in to around 6am – bliss! That is not to say that I don't enjoy the magic of 3am on a summer's day trying to find that elusive roebuck, but the longer, darker nights have a charm of their own – and certainly far more civilised hours.

It's those long summer days when you should start to formulate your doe cull. I am constantly watching where the does are and what they are doing. This monitoring is particular important during the rut, noting the locations of the young and the more mature does. We spend a lot of time on the ground and by the end of August I have a clear picture of my does and how good the retention rates are. I note the does with single kids and those with twins. We also have a smattering of triplets. If you are seeing a high number of twins or more then your current management plans, certainly in terms of deer welfare, are right. If you have too many deer on the ground you will start to note the key indicators, not least of which will be an angry landowner complaining about crop damage! A reduction in birth and retention rates and an increase in infant mortality will rapidly become evident. I also try to have an idea of which does have lost kids. Admittedly, this can be accidental. Modern farming with quick machines at the silage cut for example, or road deaths, which account for a lot of kids. A doe without kids moves up the cull list.

By the time November comes around, Tony and I will compare notes and have a good idea of where our doe cull needs to be. It is not an exact science, and a lot of factors can change things quite rapidly. You can be left with a sudden ingress of deer, or else the opposite. Some land can be vulnerable to poaching problems, particularly remote areas with quiet county roads passing through. Lamp shooting from vehicles at night can rapidly reduce your deer population, and make the culprit difficult to catch. You should be aware of these external factors, and time spent on the ground is never time wasted.

Now you have a good idea of where your deer are, the male to female ratio, and so on – so where do you start? Well, you have to start somewhere and you won't go far wrong working on the ratio of 60 per cent young to 20 per cent old and 20 per cent mature. In subsequent years it becomes easier for two main reasons: firstly, that you know the ground and your deer's behaviour patterns better, and secondly, you can monitor next year's deer sightings and numbers against this year's cull, allowing you to adjust up or down accordingly.

Perhaps one of the key bits of advice I would give is to get on with it straight away. You may think you have plenty of time but you don't! It's a short season and all manner of things can come along and get in the way: the weather can turn, game shooting interests may prevent access to woods, or crop/tree planting can disrupt your schedule to name but a few. The policy that has always stood me in good stead is to take the followers, concentrating where you can on the does with twins, and to take any does without kids. A high percentage of these will be old or yearling does. I often hear 'shoot the doe and the kid will stay and you can then shoot that as well'. It may do, but it may also run off and then you have to spend a lot of time going back to find it as it probably won't survive the winter without the guidance of the parent. Shooting the mother is a policy I don't like and, to be honest, I don't think it should form part of responsible deer management. We should be all about humane killing with the minimum chance of suffering to any animal. If you are under pressure to reduce deer numbers rapidly then it's better to account for the kids first and take the doe immediately after if the opportunity allows – and if not, then take her at a later date.

Take does without kids if you can

You must accept that the key to controlling deer and deer populations rests with the females. A lot of does will not necessarily produce more deer or more bucks. In fact, the opposite is the case. The doe season is the most important time for the deer manager and it is crucial that the right amount of effort, time and importance is attached to the task.

Some years ago I looked after a large block of conifers in a felling rotation. It was very vulnerable in terms of deer control, with blocks of new conifers being planted along with hardwoods on a regular basis. I had done the groundwork and established where a lot of the does were, as well as retention rates – all in line with my advice above. This was great until the doe season opened and all of a sudden I just couldn't find them. Apart from the odd sighting there was nothing there – rather like cocks in January, where every bird over the line is a hen.

A South Ayrshire client with his first doe

After a few trips I left the ground pretty much alone and concentrated on other plots. That was until I got a call from the forest manager in early December who was, shall we say, less then pleased. During a routine inspection and he had driven past a newly planted block in the lovely winter sunshine to see nine does with attendant followers enjoying the tips of his expensive trees. I was over that afternoon and quite shocked at the extent of the damage caused. Suffice to say, I spent a lot of time in that forest over the next month doing the job I should have done from day one! So, unless there is a specific and tangible reason to adjust your planned doe cull then stick to it or face an onslaught from an angry landowner or forest manager. Worse still, he might get someone else to do the job! **CD**

THE BIG FREEZE

I enjoy all seasons in the stalking calendar. Each brings its own problems, admittedly, but these are far outweighed by the advantages and challenges – no day is ever the same. Most recently in 2013, we had a great summer in Ayrshire (as most parts of the country did). The heat lasted long into the autumn, with very warm days right into October. The red rut started late, and the stags seemed to have no inclination to roar and chase females until late on. Who can blame them – it was 24 degrees on 29 September.

Winter stalking, therefore, was of increased importance, and I was looking forward to the colder weather, shorter days and some of the excessive vegetation dying back. I seem to have spent ages this year wading through grass and bracken up to my ears trying to find bucks – not easy. Even the stags seemed to disappear into the cover, it was that tall. At Garryloop, which is close to most of our stalking ground, we are only three miles from the coast and the Gulf stream, so our winter climate is normally very mild and frosts do not often go below minus five degrees. We don't get the severe weather or extremes of cold that have to be dealt with further north.

That said, I hadn't forgotten the cold snap that came in the first few days of April, bringing the most snow I have ever seen in Ayrshire. The isle of Arran was devastated, with drifts over 20 feet high in places, and power lines down. I think some were without electricity for more than three weeks – exceptional, admittedly, but it does happen.

It was precisely then that I had clients booked in for early bucks. They arrived full of expectation and wearing fairly light clothing. Big mistake – Arctic parkas were the order of the day. But what do you do? Well, you deal with it. The deer are there, so you simply have to work out what they will do and be there when they do it. It's difficult, if not impossible to move, especially when the top of the snow has frozen and formed that hard crust. Yes, you can walk on it, but it's like walking through a

Contrary to popular belief, the deer do show in the snow

bowl of cornflakes. If it's the soft stuff, its quieter, but you drop through it and there is a big 'swoosh' as you do it.

So usually the best policy is to really wrap up warm and sit somewhere and wait. Deer have to feed at some stage – try to find somewhere sheltered, with a bit of green visible if possible. Under these conditions I look under the edge of the conifers, out of the wind, and you will often find places where the heather or grass has been protected from the snow or, at the very least, has only a light covering. This is where the deer are most likely to be. They are reluctant to come a long way out of cover – I find they seem to realise that they stand out like the proverbial. And when they do move in the open, everything within miles can see them.

I discussed the options with my client and ensured he took into account the conditions. He still wanted to stalk rather than sit, so that's what we did. My options now were very limited – anything would hear us miles before we saw it, so I decided we would head into a larch plantation on a south-facing slope. The winds had been northerly and the snow should not have penetrated too deeply into the trees, so hopefully the frost would not have been too keen here. This was also the area where deer would have been able to access some food. All went fairly well and we were able to stalk under the trees by stepping onto any visible green clumps and carefully trying to float across the areas where the snow had settled. Good stalking, considering the conditions.

Sitting out and waiting will often see deer emerge

We made very slow but relatively quiet progress into a light breeze, and while there were loads of fresh slots and dung, we saw no deer of any sort. I was just beginning to think, "That's that, then," when my hound Oscar indicated very strongly to my left. He had clearly got a strong scent of deer. There was no mistaking the reaction – his nose was moving round like the Fylingdales early warning radar and his left leg was lifted in a half-point. I whispered to my client that we were close to deer. I needn't have bothered – he had stalked with me many times before and knew Oscar, so he had seen the indication and was looking in the direction of the dog's nose.

I trust the dog, so we go where his nose points. Very, very carefully, we moved down the slope – the problem was that this direction took us into very deep and crisp snow, and we had to cross a track through the forest, which was really compacted snow on ice. It was painstakingly slow to inch across it.

As we progressed yard by yard, the dog's reactions heightened. He was very alert now and his muscles were coiled like a spring. He kept looking back at me with that look that says, "Can't you see it yet?" No, I couldn't – no matter how hard I glassed, I could not see a deer.

We inched forward again, and then there it was: a small brown indentation in the snow. Nothing to see really, but it just did not fit the surroundings. This is the hardest thing to teach or explain to folk – it's almost a sixth sense, and a feeling

Happy hunter: Dave gets his cull buck

that something just does not fit, an ear twitch or a colour or contrast. When you have been stalking a while it just comes to you, and one of the most difficult things to do as a guide is to get the client to see what you are looking at. Sometimes they just can't see the deer, and this was the case now. We were about 45 yards away, the deer was unaware of our presence, but I just could not get my man to see what I was looking at.

Nothing for it – we had to take the bull by the horns, or the roe by the antlers. I got my man on the stick, pointed in the general direction of the deer, and warned him to be ready. I gave my best roe bark. Nothing – the buck was tucked up warm and had no intention of moving. I tried several times more and again got no response. Time for real drastic action. A snowball, nicely rolled and tossed high, landed a few feet away. That did it – up he jumped, bounded two paces and took up that classic pose, broadside on, looking back as if to say, "What was that?" By now my man had seen the buck, which was difficult to miss in snow at 50 yards, and I was about to give the 'now' command when the rifle cracked and the buck dropped on the spot.

We moved forward to where the roe had been. He had hollowed out a little shelter in soft snow, tucked out of the wind in the lee of an old larch with a small clump of blueberries at the front of the depression where he could feed without moving. Clever, and he was as snug as a bug in a rug. I never cease to be amazed at the survival instincts of these creatures.

We had a good end to a stalk in very challenging circumstances, but if I am honest, without the dog that buck would still be around today, and we would have ended a stalk with some nice, wintry, picture-postcard photographs but no venison for dinner. **CD**

BUCKING THE TREND

So after months of waiting, April rolls around. It's a time of year eagerly anticipated by all roe stalkers during the long and cold nights of winter. You've been thinking about these first forays in the early morning, with the spring flush and some warmth in the sun. And there is the anticipation of meeting that cracking buck you've been keeping tabs on – he must be a medal head this year. The more you think about it, the heavier the head gets – we have all done it.

Well, just hold fire. What should you be thinking about as that first outing approaches? When people talk about a 'roe management plan' it is usual to assume they are talking about the does, but there's no reason not to treat the bucks the same way. That said, the does do form the basis of our management at Garryloop – we want to maintain a healthy number, in balance with the type of ground they are on and at a density that does not bring them into conflict with the commercial aspect of the ground, be that timber or agricultural crops.

You don't need to worry too much about the numbers of bucks are far as females go. If your does don't come across a suitable buck on your ground, rest assured they will find one. They will even fetch him if they can't entice him to their boudoir – you can be sure of that.

But that's not to say we don't include bucks in our cull plans. We most certainly do – having taken the time and trouble to get our female population right on our areas, we do the same for the males. Ideally, we want a reasonable number of mature and dominant bucks holding territories on our ground, and to maintain that, a number of potential replacements coming through.

Photo:
Andy Lee

Young treees will be vulnerable if your management plan falls behind

Photo:
Andy Lee

You have to allow these boys room, though. They will co-habit given sufficient room to keep out of each other's way. But how often do I hear that if we leave the does alone then we will have lots of bucks next year, and if we shoot them lightly we have loads of really nice six-point bucks at the two- and three-year point? Well, you won't – you will just create a problem. The way to produce a good head is to have a balanced population of both sexes – this in turn will reduce competition for food and conflict between the deer.

The situation we face across our areas in the south-west of Scotland is that our ground is mainly commercial forestry, both broadleaf and conifer. Therefore our primary responsibility to the owners and the forestry companies who own or manage the ground we stalk is to ensure that deer damage to these trees is maintained at an acceptable level and, in particular, to protect the young and newly planted trees, which are at their most vulnerable, until they can get going. Time of year is also relevant to deer damaging trees – in winter, for example, when food can be hard to find, all deer will love a crop of tasty young shoots that a kindly forester has spent days planting for them in a lovely clear area, and they can browse away quite happily under cover of darkness.

But another key time for damage is now. The culprit is, of course, the roebuck. Firstly, we have them cleaning the velvet off their antlers, fraying and rubbing on tree branches and stems at a convenient height for the buck. At Garryloop, Anne and I like to see deer about the house, and we have landscaped the grounds. I have some seven-year-old fruit trees planted at the top of my field; half of them are now dead, their bark rubbed off, and the survivors have no lateral branches below a height of around four feet, above which they bush out like lollipops.

All this is because of buck activity, mainly in the early spring. When the antlers are clean, they begin to get really territorial and start thrashing around the same trees like a gladiator preparing for battle, marking and practising their moves ready for sorting out that young rival buck round the corner. None of this is going to make you popular with your landlord, trust me.

Action has to be taken, but your work in this department should have begun months ago. The best time for this is late winter and into early spring. Cover is down, it's cold, they need to feed and start to regain condition. Some nutrient is coming through in the form of shoots and buds, so you can find out who is about and where. You can build a picture of your dominant bucks and where the youngsters are, and get a good idea of numbers, allowing you to formulate your cull plan.

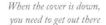

When the cover is down, you need to get out there

March is a great month for this. We shoot very little at that time – perhaps the odd follower – so while we are out maintaining seats, building towers and the like, we really get to spend time on the ground and assess the deer. So by now you know what you want to achieve in relation to the individual requirements of your own blocks and ground. You won't go far wrong following a similar cull ratio to the does: around 60 per cent young (kids born last year) to 20 per cent each old and mature.

This is very much what we do, but we do hit the youngsters hard first. That's vital, but if we see a buck of poor quality or with a poor or misshapen head, he will go too. The season will quickly move on, and these deer will learn rapidly. They are a quarry species and will become harder to find. This is compounded by the inevitable explosion of cover and bracken, and before you know it you are behind.

Later on, after they are clean, we can decide which of the better bucks to leave and which to shoot. If the numbers required for your cull remain high and your time is limited, you may not be allowed this luxury and you'll just have to take your chance as it comes. Also, other land factors may come into play – game rearing interests might require you to get the bucks sorted before July and pens are occupied, so you have to work within your own constraints.

But the key factor is to leave your dominant buck alone. He will go a long way to keeping your other bucks in order. He won't stand any nonsense from the troublemakers and will see off young bucks, and you will find your fraying damage is much reduced. If you don't think so, shoot one of your dominant bucks in early April and see the increase in fraying and territorial marking that rapidly appears on the old boy's patch as the contenders for the throne start to vie for power.

This policy works for us. A gold medal roe I shot in Ayrshire one August demonstrates this, and as explained, we are primarily involved in protecting the crop from deer.

However, the methods we use to achieve this come from sound deer management principles, and while we do not have the luxury of selecting and nurturing bucks to produce the maximum number of trophy animals at premium rates for a purely sporting estate, we are producing trophy animals and have a healthy herd.

Most of you will, I am sure, be in a similar position to us, with responsibility to a landowner for deer damage. So rather than just going out in April and shooting a buck or two, why not start to manage your deer and formulate a plan to this effect? It really is not rocket science – look at your situation, the layout of the land and factors affecting your stalking, time constraints and so on, and give it a go.

Long-term, this will improve the quality of the deer while reducing damage – and who knows, you might end up with a trophy buck on your wall. But you will certainly be countering the common argument that deer management involves seeing a deer and shooting it. So if you see that mature buck you saw by the pond last year and he is as good as you think, leave him alone and shoot the button buck round the next corner. **CD**

An obvious cull buck...

...and a happy client

RUTTING MATTERS

A medal head shot during the rut

I am sure there are not many roe stalkers out there who do not look forward to the end of July with eager anticipation: The sight of a roe doe doing a figure of eight around a tree stump, a buck following her like a steam train; calling a buck to you from deep in the woodland cover. Just a few brief weeks when normally alert and shy deer become so engrossed in matters of love that they become oblivious to all else around them, including the hunter.

The prospect of some nice weather is also welcome, although never guaranteed. Also welcome are the more sociable stalking hours (the best time to be out is often between 10am and 6pm). A lot of these romances are conducted under the cover and relative safety of darkness. Dawn breaks and the loved-up does and exhausted bucks are commonly enjoying a nap and cigarette after their exertions. So for us, it's often better to enjoy those extra few hours in bed and have a leisurely breakfast before heading out mid to late morning – the roe will have gained their second wind and be up for another go. This is also the time you are likely to catch a buck on patrol round his patch, checking that competition isn't hanging about, which is an excellent opportunity to entice it with your call. But remember there is no hard and fast rule and, if you begin thinking you can predict them, they will make a mug of you in no time. It's always worth changing your routine and trying something different.

Here in the south-west of Scotland, I find the peak of the rut will normally be early August. Looking back through my records, most success has been achieved around 5-12 August, which is probably a bit later than further south. As I go north, into Angus, I find this peak of activity is a day or two later still. It is generally accepted that rutting intensity is governed by the weather conditions at the time (as, indeed, are many things with deer). The conditions that are considered best are warm, humid and thundery weather, which are unfortunately also the conditions loved by the midge.

Save your calling until the roe have started to chase

Again, this is not to say that you won't get rutting activity in other conditions, because you will. Personally, I think the fact that sound carries a lot further in these still conditions has a lot to do with rutting bucks responding to the call – simply because they can hear it from further away.

Perhaps to illustrate how things can differ across the country, Peter, our illustrious editor, contacts me and various other outfitters across the country for an assessment of the rut each year. Here at South Ayrshire Stalking, Tony and I had a good rut last year. Bucks responded well to the call and weather conditions were favourable. However, I gather this was very much the exception. Most of the other stalkers contacted reported a poor rut, little activity and only sporadic response to calling – so you never know.

On the calls themselves and how to use them, there are many books covering this subject and excellent materials on DVDs and CDs demonstrating the different types available and methods of operation. However, nothing is better than watching and listening to someone who has mastered the art – if you get such an opportunity, grab it. It is also vital that you have a basic understanding of what you are trying, whether it is the high-pitched squeak a kid will use as a contact call for its mother, thereby drawing a doe (and hopefully an attendant buck) to you, or the agitation call a doe will make when a buck starts to press her too hard. Nothing beats actually watching and hearing these calls and the action that precedes them in the field, but you don't often get the chance.

Nothing beats watching a buck in the field

The type of call you should select is mainly down to personal choice and needs to be one you can use to make a noise vaguely resembling a deer with some degree of success. I don't think there is any harm in having a couple of different calls, but I think a pocketful is over the top. You should practise (not in the forest), and become confident in the use of your chosen call. My own preference, and certainly the call I have most success with, is the Buttolo. I find it easy to use and like that I can operate it from inside my coat pocket. I also think the muffling effect of the coat produces a good imitation. I also use a Hubertus cherry wood, which gives a nice high squeak. Again, I find it effective, and it has a slightly different tone to the Buttolo.

A buck grassed during 2012's plentiful rut

The biggest mistake folk make is that, as soon as July approaches, out of the drawer comes the call and off into the wood goes the stalker, calling in earnest. All you are doing is educating the deer – and they quickly realise that something odd is going on. Practice all you like, but make sure you are nowhere near roe. You are much more likely to succeed if you wait until you have seen some rutting activity, and if you stick to the period around the last week in July and the first two weeks in August you should be around the right time.

I distinctly recall, a good few years ago, travelling from Yorkshire to my stalking ground close to Newton Stewart. On the way I was listening to a tape (one of those old things you used to put in a car cassette player) of Richard Prior demonstrating excellent use of a Buttolo. Having listened to this several times during my drive through the night, and arriving close to my ground a bit early, I pulled into a layby, got the flask out and, while having a coffee, practised my best technique on the Buttolo. I was so engrossed in my attempts to replicate a female roe that I didn't notice the lorry pull into the layby, but jumped half out of my skin at the tap on the window and polite question from a trucker enquiring if I was all right. It was quite difficult to explain why I was sitting in a layby at 2.30am, squeezing a little black rubber thing. You have been warned! **CD**

AYRSHIRE CALLING

The anticipation of 'the rut' is certainly infectious for all who follow the sport. It's also invariably a time when lots of stalkers ask me about which calls I use, how I use them, where and when. Many drop into the conversation that they have been out in woods practising their calling for a few weeks already. I just shake my head. Don't do it! All you are doing is educating the deer with little chance of any response. Roe deer do not respond well to some human wandering around and squeaking, trying to make like a fawn. You will just push them into cover and make them all the more wary – better to leave them quiet until rutting behaviour is evident.

The rut in not an exact science. It will happen, but some years, owing to many factors, usually the weather, we see little of it, with most of the activity taking place at night. Secondly, peak activity can occur in a long period of perhaps four weeks, usually from mid-July to mid-August and sometimes beyond. This can also vary massively between areas; normally I would expect rutting in the south of England to be 2-3 weeks earlier than here in the south-west of Scotland, but this is not always the case. Take last year, for example – we had a near-perfect rut with deer responding well to calls, but this was by far the exception.

Chris works with the Buttolo call

So what do I do? Well I don't start calling until I have seen some rutting activity and I already have a good idea of what bucks and does I have, and their locations. Watch your mature bucks, and at the same time note any pretenders to the throne, along with any nervous yearlings. Also, ring the changes of your stalking. During the rut, it's often better to get out mid-morning to mid-afternoon. A second burst of rutting behaviour will often take place around this time – the deer are often laid up after dawn after strenuous activity during the night.

The two calls I prefer are the Buttolo and the Hubertus cherry wood. I keep trying the Nordic Roe, but with the latter I seem to struggle – I just can't yet make a consistent noise but others swear by it.

Do not go into the woods expecting instant success. You will invariably be disappointed. But persevere, and by following the basic pointers above you will be narrowing the odds. When you first get to your chosen calling position, wait a while before calling. The disturbance of your arrival alone may be enough to bring in a buck in close proximity who may think you are an interloper – if you have the wind. And when you do start calling, be aware that a wary buck may try to come in from behind to test the wind if he's a cautious one – and the bigger bucks usually are. When you eventually succeed it is magic – calling your first buck is something you will never forget.

Last year, a regular stalking guest asked me to take out his son Tom during early August, and try calling a decent roebuck for him. Our first morning saw me drive to a farm with some small conifers that had been planted with

Photo: Shutterstock

pheasant shooting in mind. This is great roe terrain – big open valleys bounded by conifers and hardwoods, which is also ideal for calling. You can quietly get into some high ground with a great view across both sides of the glen.

I had been watching this particular spot and noted a decent six-point buck hanging around a doe. She was not particularly interested but nor was she getting stroppy with him, so having given it a few days, I thought there was a good chance of things having progressed in the amour department. I had seen several rutting chases on this estate already, so females were certainly coming into season.

The weather was warm and a bit breezy, which kept the midges off. We were in position around 9am. I settled Tom down and we got into a comfortable calling position, trees behind us and the rifle rested on the sticks ready for action.

I sat for 10 minutes to let everything settle down and took time to glass the area carefully. The new Swarovski EL Range binos are great for ranging various references points. Nothing apparent, so I gave three gentle peeps on the Buttolo, squeezing the call from the inside my coat pocket to give a gentler, more realistic note.

I had not even finished the third 'peep' when a lovely six-pointer dashed out of the trees 500 yards above us and stood looking intently in our direction. Roe have an uncanny knack of being able to pinpoint the exact location of a noise. Experience told me he couldn't see us, but I felt I was being stared at. I nudged Tom but he had seen the buck already and was slowly, as briefed, bringing the rifle round to the buck.

At this instant the buck ran at us full tilt down the valley, to disappear out of sight below us. This allowed Tom time to get into a good rest and I pointed to where I thought the buck would re-appear on our side of the Glen. This he duly did, still running at top speed; he was now in danger of getting too close, so I whispered to Tom to be ready and I barked at the buck. He slammed on the anchors and turned beautifully broadside to a halt. The bullet hit him fair and square, knocking him to the ground dead.

The whole thing, from start to finish, probably lasted no more than two minutes. I wish it was always like that – more often it's a no show, but boy, when it does work it's great. Be observant, know where your bucks are, practise your calling at home or in the car, and be ready to take a quick but safe shot. Good luck. **CD**

Photo:
Andy Lovel

PROSPERITY'S IN THE PLANNING

Get to know your stalking land and its uses

When the buck season draws to an end, it's time to tackle the next big challenge: planning the winter cull. Many of my stalking guests ask me what I think is the best way to achieve a good balance of females on the many areas I control. There are a few answers I give, but ultimately, the issue is subjective – not an exact science. It is also a broad question and very much dependent upon circumstances and the type and use of your stalking ground. By this I mean the lie of the land, who is using it, whether there are game interests or if it is agricultural land, how often you can stalk there and whether it is broadleaf or conifer – open glades or narrow rides. These are some of the questions you must ask before you can decide on a plan that works for you.

Long before 1 November you will (or should) have assessed the density of deer on the ground – a subject that we could all write a book on, so I won't try to cover it here in a few short paragraphs. Let's assume you currently have a density of deer that seems about right, and by that I mean you are seeing deer but there are no issues with unacceptable levels of deer damage to crops or trees, and your landowner is not complaining about the systematic destruction of his newly planted oaks or winter turnips. Let's also assume you have a stable deer population and numbers are not increasing or decreasing year on year, and you are shooting roughly the same numbers when you look back on your cull data (make sure you keep accurate cull details, it's essential). When assessing such data, look at the frequency of your stalking. A career change that means you can only get to the ground once a month will affect your cull, so don't overlook this when comparing cull achievement against last year's figures.

You also have to recognise that controlling the females is the key to a stable and balanced roe population. I've heard folk say far too often that they don't shoot many does as they want a lot of bucks the following year. This is completely flawed logic and not the attitude of a responsible deer manager. You must sort out your does and, having accepted that, work out how to go about it.

Get on with it as soon as you can. I hear the comment, "I could have shot three last month but I want some to shoot in February so I just shot one." You need to get on top of your cull as soon as you are able to and when the chance is offered. Many times the opportunity will not present itself again; the doe and twin kids you saw easily in early November have gone in late December, as have the other doe and twins you saw in the hardwood plantation. In all probability they are still around somewhere but feeding in a different area, at different times

Photo:
Andy Lovel

It's the followers that are primarily taken

Know your numbers and take the roe when you can

or under cover of darkness. You get to late March and the spring growth starts, daylight hours lengthen and all of a sudden all the does and followers reappear along with a few family groups you were not aware of. You now have a problem as most of your mature does will also be carrying a new batch of young that will be born in a few months' time. You are about to experience a major population increase and subsequent grief from your landowner at the resulting deer damage, notwithstanding the potential problems for the deer caused by a rapid population growth and subsequent competition for space and food.

I am fortunate that Tony and I can assess the areas we look after frequently and have a good idea of what is happening. I have regular, experienced syndicate stalkers who know the ground well and are my eyes and ears. We have a detailed and accurate cull record so I know what the cull needs to be and I can monitor its effectiveness. We also operate mainly in areas where other disturbance is minimal and don't have a lot of ground that, for example, is also used for game shooting with the subsequent possible conflict in shooting interests. The keeper does not want you stalking through his best coverts and release pens at dusk just as the birds are going to roost. A shot from a high velocity rifle and the birds will be pushed off their roost and fly down to the floor – you will not be popular with the keeper but the resident fox will appreciate it. We do have disturbance, of course, such as timber extraction and replanting, but you can work round that and it's all the more reason to get on with your cull when you can.

As a general rule, if you work on the accepted practice of around 60 per cent young (followers) to around 20 per cent each of old and mature, you shouldn't go far wrong. To achieve this, my stalkers and guests are instructed to always take a follower and leave the mature doe alone. Depending on the cull requirements and if the opportunity arises, they may take both followers. If, however, we encounter a lone and mature doe, after a period of observation to ensure she has no followers, we will take her. By adopting this method I find that my cull ratio always fits very closely to the 60:20:20 split. Furthermore, I do not leave young kids to fend for themselves through the winter period – they may survive, but will benefit and have a much better survival rate under the guidance of the doe. By culling does with no kids you are probably also removing older animals that have not bred or that have lost kids for whatever reason, so again these are the animals to remove. I do not like the practice of shooting the mother with an expectation that the kid may hang around or come back after running off and then you can shoot it. This does sometimes happen but surely it is better to take the kid and to take the mature doe at a later time if needed.

Enjoy the social side of your winter stalking – you don't have to get up at silly o'clock to be back home in time to enjoy a meal and a beer. But remember, if you are not on top of your winter doe cull by the time February ends, you are running late (stalkers on shooting estates excepted, and I sympathise). **CD**

THE GREEN MILE

You will probably have gathered by now that quite a lot of my writing stems discussions over dinner at Garryloop after a stalking outing. Conversation usually flows after a full day in the forest, a nice meal and a glass or two of wine. I work on the principle that if my guests are interested in these topics then other folk will be as well.

Another subject that generated a long debate was roe's reaction to a shot and subsequent follow up, and how many deer that 'run on' are actually recovered. This brought to mind a doe I shot in January 2013.

It is unusual these days for me to be out with the rifle. Most of the time I am talking other people out or witnessing for DSC Level 2, so for me to be stalking alone is out of the ordinary. One of the areas we look after has recently been clear felled and a large area replanted during the last few months, so the

The rain kept stalking opportunities to a minimum

deer required close control. I had stalked there with clients several times over previous weeks, mainly with guests who were doing an introduction to stalking course, and had seen four or five family groups of roe in the area. For various reasons we had accounted for only two roe followers on these outings, mainly because of my guests' inexperience. Roe in winter coat on a restock site are difficult to see even for the experienced hunter. Add that to unfamiliarity with handling a rifle, and how long it takes to get ready before taking a shot. None of this is their fault and we all have to learn.

I was acutely aware that, with a cold snap forecast, a few more of these roe needed to be removed from the area. As a free evening coincided with a lull in the rain, I went out. The ground has a steep hillside on which conifers and a few areas of hardwood have been planted across a total plot of around 1,300 acres. This was bounded on one side by a track and some conifers planted seven years ago, while on the other side there was a belt of mature conifers close to felling. The hill caught the afternoon sun and was always a good place to try in the evenings. Deer would often lie out in the trees on a warm day, and if not you could catch them coming out to feed in the evening from the trees at either side.

On this evening there was a brisk and cold wind blowing across the slope to the mature conifers at the top of the hill. It was coming from a quarter that would allow me to stalk in between the mature trees and the replanted site at the top of the slope. I stalked carefully along this edge and glassed the slope every few paces as a new vista came into view. It's a tactic I have used before often with good success but not on this occasion. The dog indicated once and had obviously winded deer but I could not see anything.

Roe are masters of blending in with their own habitat. Photo: Andy Lee

At the end of the plantation the ground dropped away into a sheltered valley that was tucked out of the wind. In front of me was a quiet glen and mossy bank that just felt right. I recall thinking to myself, 'If I were a roe, this is where I would be tonight,' so I found a tree stump and settled down to wait. I had been there for 30 minutes and put the glasses up for the umpteenth time, scanning across the bank. Browsing quite contentedly was a doe 250 yards away. How many times has that happened? She was 25 yards from cover in full view. How long had she been there? Roe are commonly called the elves of the forest and the more I stalk the more I realise why.

I glassed her for a while and established that she was an old doe with no follower, meaning she was in the plan and could go. I walked forward slowly along the tree line, moving only when she did or was busy feeding, then freezing when her head came up to look round. The wind concerned me a bit, as it was drifting a little too close to her direction for comfort. I had reached an upturned tree root at about 140 yards and that's as close I dared go. Any further forward and I would have been in plain view.

I set up the rifle on the sticks from a kneeling position and waited for the broadside. For a long time she continued to work down the bank but would not present the shot. I felt a gust of wind on my neck and her head went up – she had winded me, nose testing the air and looking intently in my direction. Stiff-legged, she began to turn. Fortunately, she was still curious and paused for a look back. This gave me a safe broadside shot, and I heard the satisfying crack of the strike. I caught sight of her dashing right and then she was gone down the bank.

The dog was looking at me expectantly, but as always we waited, allowing things to settle down and any other deer to move off – you gain nothing by rushing. After 10 minutes we moved forward and I was expecting to see the doe lying dead around the corner. However, after an initial search I could find nothing. No paint or pins, and I couldn't see the deer. Puzzled, I sent Oscar, my Weimaraner, to find her.

Oscar did not need asking twice. Head down, he moved forward and finally, after about 45 yards, we had a nice blood trail and a little further on a large piece of lung. Relieved, I fully expected the dog to come on to the deer in a few yards. But no, he continued on his determined hunt, nose down through the trees in a long loop, out the other side, over a stream and towards some trees almost 200 yards away. I called him back, a little miffed that he was messing about. Taking him back to the bit of lung, I cast him off again with the instructions 'where is it' and 'steady', his command to seek a deer in cover.

He gave me one of those looks and followed exactly the same line he did before. I still couldn't believe the deer had run all that way, but I trusted him and set off in pursuit. I really should know better by now, but 45 yards further on from where I called him back, there was the doe lying dead under some thick young conifers.

When I measured the distance, the doe had made 247 yards from a perfect heart and lung shot. In so doing it had crossed a small stream twice, run a loop through some conifers, gone across a valley and ended up in a thick block of trees. Without a dog, I would never have recovered her. After searching in completely the wrong place, I would still be puzzling about it now.

I have recovered thousands of shot deer over the years and I often find myself watching deer as a client shoots them and see first-hand their reaction to the shot. While I knew she had winded me and was ready to run, I would never have imagined she could have got so far. **CD**

A 247-yard follow-up – unbelievable but a reality

LOST DEER

Having been called out with my Weimaraner Oscar to recover a shot deer one of my syndicate stalkers couldn't find, I was reminded of a few days one February when I had both missed and lost deer on successive outings – which is unusual to say the least! The missed deer occurred during some DSC 2 witnessed stalks for an experienced hunter for the Netherlands. He had what appeared to be two relatively easy shots on successive mornings, and completely missed both times. The next day I was required to go out twice with Oscar to search for two roe that were hit hard and ran into conifers.

Now, I have said many times before that we all miss, but this should be the exception rather than the rule. If you are missing on any other than the rarest occasions, then you are doing something wrong. So to have a situation with four incidents in a week is most unusual, and I can't remember it happening before or since. My visitor from Holland was a very experienced hunter and proved an excellent shot on the range. So the only explanation I could offer for his misses was the fact that he was keen to complete his DSC 2 and, having the opportunity to get off to a good start with two deer in two outings, and possibly having someone watching from behind, put just enough pressure on him to miss shots at roe that he would usually have taken without thinking. The furthest could only have been around 80 yards from a stable position. These were clear misses; full searches with trained dogs revealed nothing, and the deer were observed running off for some distance, clearly none the worse for wear.

The 'misses' that Oscar subsequently located and I recovered, however, are an entirely different matter – and one I think makes a good teaching point for us all. Derek, one of my regular stalking guests from Yorkshire, had arrived the day before and, unusually for me, I had decided to go along with him to a large area of Forestry Commission ground for a morning stalk. I don't get much chance to do this these days as I am usually taking other folk out, so the prospect of being chauffeured to the forest and having an outing with my rifle for a change was too good to miss.

I let Derek pick his area and I went the other way, agreeing a time to meet back at the vehicle. My morning was spent carefully stalking down

Tracking a deer in thick cover is not easy. You need to know the ground well

98   ROE STALKING WITH THE EXPERTS

some spectacular open gullies on the edge of the Galloway Forest Park, and while I always enjoy being out in these remote and quiet places early on, it was nevertheless a frustrating morning. One of those days when the wind is always wrong, or the deer not in season, and the one roe follower I could have taken just would not move from an unsafe position where she was skylined. Her mother, on the other hand, spent 20 minutes fully broadside to me and then lay down.

While I stood considering my options, the sound of a distant shot rang out and, as it was approaching time to return to the vehicle, I set off back, expecting to meet Derek there with his dinner for the next week in tow. Wrong! When I got to the Land Rover Derek was waiting, and explained that he had missed a follower but he couldn't understand how. We discussed it, and I was debating going back with the dog, but he was convinced he had missed as there was no evidence of a strike, no reaction to the shot, no telltale sound, and his search under the trees revealed nothing. We concluded that, as the shot was downhill, he might have pulled it and probably missed over the top of the roe.

Back at Garryloop, while eating breakfast I just had a nagging feeling that something was wrong. I decided to go back with Oscar to have a look. What bothered me was that Derek was initially happy with the shot. Usually I find that when you have been stalking a while you know if the shot was good or not, and if there is any chance of a deer being hit I would rather check than just assume. I would take the rifle and sit for the last hour anyway, as we still needed a few roe followers to finish the cull. Following Derek's route from earlier that morning, Oscar stiffened and his nose went into the air, pointing right towards a cross ride in front of me. I recognised that sign, and knew he had smelled deer, so I sat him and stalked slowly forward. Sure enough, a doe and two followers were browsing across in front of me. I took the doe follower, gralloched her and left her hanging in a small broadleaf to collect on my way back up the Glen. I much prefer the suspended gralloch, and this is the method we teach all of our DSC 2 candidates. It's so much easier than the gralloch on the floor.

From here, it was not far to the point where Derek had missed his roe. About 15 minute later I gave Oscar the instruction to search, and he worked his way

Photos above and below: Andy Lee

Oscar and Chris work as a partnership to bring the deer back

under the trees. He was immediately interested and snuffled slowly forward. I followed him and after about 150 yards we came to the doe – so not a miss after all. The strike was slightly forward and low, but in the low lung area, and the deer had made around 30 yards from the strike point to where it now lay dead. I am slightly puzzled as to why Derek had not found her, but it was a good result and I returned to where my own roe hung. I had a long carry back up the glen with two roe. I am very glad of the Apex predator roe sack I use, and I can confirm that yes, you can fit two roe in it – just!

Back at Garryloop I found a very dejected Derek, who explained that he had shot at but lost another doe that evening – one he was sure he had hit. Again much discussion ensued, and after Derek had taken me through the deer's reaction to the shot, I was almost sure the shot was good. The deer should not be far from the strike point. By now Derek was unusually quiet and, while slightly bolstered by my finding the first deer, seemed troubled by the events of the evening. A wee dram marginally helped, but his refusal of a second helping of my wife Anne's excellent herb and parmesan crusted rainbow trout told me the situation was serious.

We were off again at first light the next morning, and again Oscar earned his wages. Initially, as we were searching in the wrong place, he showed little interest, but after I cast him off to where Derek had marked the strike, he immediately got his nose down. I noted blood and some small sections of lung: the doe was about 30 yards further on under the trees. Examination revealed a perfect heart-lung shot.

So remember, the follow-up of a shot deer must be thorough and systematic, and you need to search a large area. Even well-hit deer can cover quite some ground, and this can be extended further if you wrongly mark the deer's position. And never assume a miss, even if you see no obvious sign or reaction to the shot. I have watched deer through the binos on a number of occasions when a client has shot them and have seen no reaction, but recovered a dead deer shortly after.

Derek left that week with a lesson learned, and I got to thinking: was this all a clever ploy on his part? Shoot two roe a long carry away from the car, pretend you can't find them, and send your stalking guide out with his dog to fetch them for you? Now I wonder! Having said that, the two bottles of Scotland's finest and two full Wensleydale cheeses that arrived a few weeks later made it worthwhile. **CD**

PETER CARR

Peter Carr is one of the most prolific writers and editors on the sporting circuit. He is an award-winning editor of sporting publications, holding editor-in-chief roles on *Sporting Rifle* and *Modern Gamekeeping* magazines and a dual presenter-director role on The Shooting Show. In 2011 he authored *The British Deer Stalking Bible*, which quickly sold out and saw a second edition published. Following this he produced an updated edition of Hesketh Prichard's legendary *Sport in Wildest Britain*, hitherto long out of print, in 2014. This new edition pairs Prichard's unparalleled writing with Pete's modern perspective on Prichard's hunts and includes four new chapters, effectively making two books in one. He has also co-authored several collections of hunting and shooting expertise in book form, including *Sporting Rifles* and *Foxing With The Experts*.

Pete describes himself as a keen hunter-conservationist, and through *Sporting Rifle* has helped raise over £25,000 for Save the Rhino to combat poaching in South Africa. But the species closest to his heart is the humble roe deer, and it is to this species that he has devoted more written words than any other. Stalking mainly on Yorkshire estates and farms, with significant time spent chasing roe in the Scottish Highlands, he has made the subject his own.

He is an experienced stalker and big game hunter, and a sometimes controversial but always sporting writer. He has hunted extensively in the UK and Ireland, and has taken all the species still open to the British sportsman, and though he spent a long stint hunting dangerous game in Africa and outfitting safaris, he still views the roe as his favourite quarry.

UNCERTAIN ORIGINS

The roe deer (*Capreolus capreolus*) must be the mainstay quarry species for most British stalking enthusiasts. I have been fortunate enough to hunt a great variety of animals worldwide, but my personal favourite species is still the roebuck. The excitement when I take to the field in pursuit of this quarry remains as strong as it was the first day I weaved through a hawthorn hedge and grassed my debut buck with an inferior calibre. Thankfully, I soon progressed to a more suitable choice of rifle and fell under the wing of such stalkers as Stuart Donald, Steve Kershaw and Mark Brackstone, who showed me the error of my ways.

Roe doe: The fairy of the woods

For reasons mostly unknown, the species enjoyed a huge population explosion during the second half of the 20th century. Modern forestry and farming have suited the roe deer well and have definitely contributed to its expansion in both numbers and range. During the 1970s in my part of East Yorkshire, I remember the sighting of a roe deer as a very rare occurrence, but today it is commonplace.

The mostly indigenous northern population is spreading rapidly southwards, with roe now beginning to become established in the Midlands – the last tract of England yet to be colonised by this deer other than Kent. The Midlands will be, without doubt, where the northern and southern populations of roe deer will coexist in the near future. Roe deer are extremely common today throughout Scotland and England (except for the two areas just noted), and are currently expanding into Wales at an astonishing rate.

Roebuck: Still Britain's most sought-after deer

This, however, hasn't always been the case, and many readers may be surprised to learn that less than a century ago the roe deer was rare in our Isles. Interestingly, the indigenous English population had all but died out at the beginning of the 19th century. Even as early as the reign of Charles I, roe were extremely scarce in the southern counties. Records show that Charles bought 31 roe kids for £7 12s 6d from Naworth Castle, Cumberland, to turn out in Half-Moon Park, Wimbledon, Surrey.

Forest clearance and excessive persecution in the early 19th century led to the extinction of roe deer across pretty much all of England, with just a few surviving in the Lake District and possibly two remnant populations at Cannock Chase and Petworth Park. Even in Scotland, this species was at one point restricted to the Highlands and a few sporadic populations further south.

During research for my latest book, I charted the remarkable reintroduction of this species and its subsequent spread back into its former range, and also turned up some interesting anomalies. It is commonly believed that the roe was completely absent in the south of England at the turn of the 19th century, but this may not be quite true. The Normans introduced some roe from the northern counties to Cannock Chase in Staffordshire. These were thought to

have gone by the turn of the 20th century, but it appears that they had not. These forgotten roe have slowly populated the surrounding area in more recent times and will shortly be joined by the two separate British populations as they colonise the Midlands from both the north and the south.

Further introductions to Sussex and Dorset were possibly made by the Earl of Egremont with roe from Scandinavian stock bought at Brook's Menagerie, London, in the 1780s. Others at Milton Abbas, Dorset, were presented to Lord Dorchester, again by Lord Egremont and probably Lord Portarlington in the early 1800s. The latter's stock was said to be sourced from Perthshire – though this has been disputed. These animals were initially introduced to provide sport for the local buckhounds, which hunted them up to 1829. A number of these roe were later moved to Charborough Park, where conditions obviously suited them. This population thrived, and soon expanded eastwards into the New Forest and westwards to colonise Dartmoor, Exmoor and as far north as the Marquis of Bath's woodlands at Longleat in Wiltshire.

Thetford Forest is the stronghold of the species in the east of England. This thriving population owes its establishment to William Dalziel Mackenzie, who released a number of German roe imported from Württemberg on to his Santon Downham Estate, Norfolk in 1884. Within 20 years these roe had spread more than 15 miles from their original release site and were well established in the surrounding countryside.

In 1897 and again in 1910, the then Duke of Bedford released a few of the largest of the three roe sub-species, the Siberian roe (*Capreolus capreolus pygargus*) to run freely at Woburn Park, Bedfordshire. This sub-species is much bigger in both body weight and antler than the European roe (*Capreolus capreolus*), and as such quite easily identifiable. These animals quickly established themselves in the estate woodlands, and at the nearby Ampthill Forest. By 1938, Siberian roe were reported across the Northamptonshire border, in both Hazelborough and Yardley forests some 20 miles away. Other sightings from Salcey Forest on the Buckinghamshire border told of a definite expansion.

Unfortunately, during and immediately after World War Two, the Woburn population had declined to no more than three or four individuals because of poaching, no doubt due to wartime rationing restrictions. This decline was echoed elsewhere, and only a few lingered on in Salcey and Ampthill forests. During the next decade, sporadic sightings attributed to the Siberian sub-species came in from the East Midlands, Oxfordshire and the Home Counties. The only definite record of a Siberian being shot more than 20 miles from Woburn was the

beast taken by Brian Vesey-Fitzgerald at Inkpen, Berkshire, in March 1948. However, it would be fair to say that any roe sighted in the Midlands before their extinction by 1960 would probably be of the Siberian sub-species.

Scottish roe have mostly increased from native stock, although the south-west population was mainly achieved by introduction (this is disputed by Whitehead, who believed the eastern lowlands were mainly colonised by surviving native roe still living in Lanarkshire woodlands). However, it is known that the Marquis of Bute introduced some roe to his Culzean Estate in Ayrshire at the beginning of the 19th century. Finding conditions extremely favourable, these roe quickly spread eastwards and eventually met another expanding population, introduced to Nithsdale around 1860 by the Duke of Buccleuch and Queensberry at his Drumlanrig Castle Estate.

Wales has recently seen the return of the roe deer, where it has been extinct for centuries. In the mid-1980s the species pushed across the English border into Wales in the Mortimer Forest area. Roe now occupy much of the land from the English border westwards to the Cardigan area, stopping just short of the coast and as far north as Bangor.

A damaged willow wand frayed by a buck

In Ireland, roe deer have a brief but illustrious history. The species was never indigenous to the country, but a few were liberated at Lissadell, Co Sligo, and appeared initially to do quite well. Some of these bucks later produced enormous multipoint heads, which are still the talk of trophy enthusiasts. These roe originated from Dupplin Castle, Perthshire (an area that continues to produce quality trophies today), and were liberated at Lissadell Estate in the early 1870s by Sir Henry Gore-Booth Bt. These roe survived for half a century and a few spread into Co Mayo, but they were never very numerous despite a later attempt to supplement stock. After the area was planted with forestry, the deer damage wasn't tolerated, and the species was quickly shot out of existence and disappeared from Ireland completely.

A red-letter outing at the bucks. Photos above and below: Sean Scott

There is no doubt that the fate of this species has been reversed in a dramatic manner. Many reasons are probably responsible for this, but there can be little doubt that all the reasons originate at the hand of man.

As sporting a quarry as the species is, it mustn't be forgotten that roe deer can unfortunately cause significant damage to forestry by reducing tree regeneration, browsing saplings, and fraying intensively. Actual economic losses in forestry due to roe deer are hard to quantify, but overall management costs are much more easily assessed. The amount spent by the Forestry Commission in Scotland alone runs into millions of pounds a year.

As stalkers both amateur and professional, we have a duty to manage our burgeoning roe population and do our best to prevent damage to forestry and farming interests. There are already murmurs from the unenlightened who would press for unethical forms of control and unnecessary shooting season extensions to halt the spread of all UK deer. It would certainly be a very sad day indeed to see the status of the roe deer downgraded to that of a pest species – it is up to us to ensure that never happens. **PC**

OPENING DAY

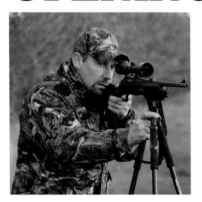

It's no secret that my favourite rifle quarry is the roebuck. In second place is the African leopard – that should give you a yardstick as to how highly I value this sporting species. The roebuck is the bread and butter of most UK stalkers, Highlanders excepted. The southern counties England of course hold the premier trophies, but it shouldn't be forgotten that Scotland's Fife and Perthshire regularly produce outstanding heads, too, as do other counties. In my area of East Yorkshire there are good bucks to be taken each year, and as stalking is one of our fastest growing fieldsports I expect more and more counties of England not so well known for big bucks to start to produce.

The first of April is more than just a day to play practical jokes on friends and colleagues. For roe stalkers it is the start of a new season, and its approach always excites me. What will the season bring, I always wonder. Will the bucks produce good heads, and will this year be the one that I can fill a slot on my bucket list for a once-in-anyone's-lifetime freaky head. Not a spark has diminished in my pursuit of roe since I crawled down that slurry ditch some 30 years ago to secure my first buck.

Last year was no exception. I had watched and spied an ageing buck with a poor head living close to a busy junction. The morning of the opening day arrived, and saw me silently waiting beneath a budding hawthorn hedge with the busy commuter traffic whizzing by behind me. The shadows had receded and I was carefully checking the hedgerows through the Swarovski binos. Cramp seems to affect me much more now since I passed the big four-zero, and I was twiddling my toes to aid the circulation. I knew my best course of action was to stay put, but my backside had gone to sleep and I was fast becoming sick of the cramps, so in a less than graceful manner I rose to my feet.

The fox nearly became the stalk's new quarry

I had the wind, of course, and I proceeded to walk and stalk at as slow a pace as I possibly could, stopping and spying as I went on. Imagine my consternation when moments later the buck pushed its way through the hedge 50 yards away to my left and looked directly at me. If I had just stayed in my sitting position a few moments longer, he would have been in my sight glass, but now I was made. Keeping still was my only option, but I stood out like a turd on a billiard table.

The buck licked his nose, searching for any hint of scent. He craned his neck from side to side, trying to make out what this apparition was before him. I'm sure the Mossy Oak camo helped me blend in well with the adjacent hawthorn hedge, but I was still a suspicious object, and the buck decided that flight was the better part of valour and disappeared across the field and onto the neighbouring estate.

That, as they say, was that. I stalked down the boundary and waited in a suitable spot for his return but gave up the ghost at 9am. Returning home for breakfast, I found I'd left my brand new Rivers West ball cap at my last position, and thought nothing more of it. Returning in the late afternoon, I was just getting my kit out of the Land Rover when a trio of mountain bikers sped by the lay-by – with one of them wearing my new cap. Despite me demanding them to halt, they carried on in what could be best described as good humour, ignoring my calls questioning their parentage. Fortunately I usually carry a spare, and I donned an SCI cap given to me by an American client.

Grabbing the sticks, I set off in dark mood to my previous position to await the buck's return. The buck proved to be a will-o-the-wisp as no sooner had I reached my destination than he reappeared out of the dyke beside me and skipped away down the hedge – but alas, over the boundary. I felt sure he hadn't been disturbed despite his closeness, as he didn't appear particularly alarmed. But boundaries are boundaries, and I elected to stay and wait for what if anything would transpire.

The buck finally reappeared, and Pete made the most of it

Minutes ticked by, and as always, nature's soap opera kept me entertained as a love triangle of wrens battled it out in the hedgerow beside me. The piping of a blackbird put me on the alert, and sure enough a fox came towards me on a reciprocal course to the one taken by the buck. I knew the keeper next door would be pleased with this result, so I flicked on the illuminated dot on the Swarovski and mounted the Sauer.

Through the scope the buck then came into view from nowhere and blocked out the fox. My intended quarry slipped into the dyke once more, and I lowered the rifle like a fool. This movement was instantly picked up by the fox, who turned away and took the buck's lead into the dyke.

With my mood rapidly blackening, I was just about to give up when the buck came into view at my side of the hedge and stood there, weighing me up. It was another Mexican standoff. The Sauer 202 rifle came instantly to the shoulder, and I flicked off the safety and squeezed away the round as the reticle came up to the beast's shoulder. The buck had begun to turn away, but the Geco .30-06 bullet flew true and knocked the beast to the ground dead in an instant.

It had been a testing day, but what a start to the season. The Sauer-Swarovski combination had proved itself, and some sharp thinking and tricky shooting had secured a fine start to the new season. I've said it once and I'll say it again – you cannot beat the excitement of roe stalking, culling or trophy hunting. This species is the one that does it for me. **PC**

OPERATION ROE DOE

With a small window to achieve cull numbers, a group effort is called for.
Photo: Andy Lee

Every estate has, or should have, a cull plan for its deer herd. Normally it is imperative to shoot more females than males within that plan to keep the health and growth of the herd in check. However it is usually easier to take out the males for a variety of reasons. Many a deer manager will relate to this, and just as many again will have felt the pressure of having to attain the required cull figure with the season's end fast approaching. Even amateur stalkers with their own ground will have a cull plan to adhere to and again the cause for concern will be culling enough females.

Typically, trophy hunters will put the time in during the buck season, for obvious reasons. Unless they are particularly partial to venison they may be unwilling to spend as much time on the does. In the course of my work I have met many stalkers who profess that they are not trophy hunters, but very few who were unwilling to take a trophy animal if a shot was offered and none who did not want to keep the antlers afterwards.

Personally, I like both trophies and venison but prefer stalking in the winter months as this is the time of year when I am unhindered by clients and the associated pressures of finding them a suitable buck. Roe doe stalking is terrific value for money, and letting out a few days is a useful way of attaining your cull in a short space of time while adding a few coins to the kitty.

I used to manage the stalking on a wonderful little roe forest in the Angus Glens on the Glen Trusta estate. It was on the edge of the Highlands and marched with a well-stocked grouse moor that teemed with mountain hares and had some super stag stalking in the rut. Glen Trusta was a real gem of a roe forest and was also known as the windy glen, for good reason.

Commercial letting was the order of the day there as it was a private estate and had to make itself pay. A beautiful trout loch stocked with a variety of game fish and rough shooting were well-established and making money. The stalking was untapped at that time and I was brought in to manage the burgeoning roe population – and what an opportunity it was.

It was obvious from the first buck season that there were too many deer on the ground as their body weights were extremely light compared to the deer that resided on neighbouring estates. Hitting the required cull target was certainly cause for concern and required some serious planning. What I decided to do has stood me in good stead ever since.

Geographically, Glen Trusta was a problem as I was based in Yorkshire. Winter weather considerations were another major problem during the doe season, and this meant I had a relatively small window to achieve my cull numbers. In the first year I had only taken six females and time was running out. I decided to hit them hard towards the season's close with a group who I could trust to shoot well, as clean carcases were imperative for the game dealer.

Roe quickly get wise to being moved to rifles. Photo: Andy Lee

It goes without saying that you would need to know your ground well, and I had a number of well-placed high seats dotted around the estate that had proved their worth in the buck season. I was going to work the estate in a number of sections over a long weekend in an attempt to address the situation across the area.

This entailed the use of six rifles, placed in high seats, and one man with dog who would stalk the covered block carefully with the wind before working it back slowly and quietly, keeping the dog close in an attempt to move – and not drive – the deer towards the rifles in ambush. All deer are alerted by the scent of a dog.

Silence is crucial when placing clients in high seats and can make the difference between failure and success. This is even more apparent when several people are involved in a particular operation such as this.

We headed out into the forestry well before dawn, left the vehicles at the estate entrance and split into two teams to keep noise to a minimum. Chris Whyke, who would be the stalker, took two rifles with him and I, who had furthest to go, took one with me. Everybody was eventually in position and, after I left my charge safely ensconced in his seat, the paling eastern sky heralded the approaching sunrise. The temperature dropped a degree or two, as it does in the pre-dawn, and coupled with the damp conditions it caused each niggle and injury to ache like hell. The pre-arranged start couldn't come soon enough.

A sharp report in the distance announced first blood and that the deer were on the move.

Chris carefully stalked the rides and glades into the wind with the hound at heel. Occasional shots sounded promising; I just hoped that they were not all directed at foxes. I had considered putting a ban on shooting them during the exercise but decided against it as to pass up on shooting Reynard is a tall order on an estate with game shooting concerns.

The Basset bleu de Gascogne: An ideal choice for moving roe

The 12ft stands of sitka spruce and Douglas fir stood before me. All was quiet apart from an intermittent rifle report and the odd *kronk, kronk* of the raven as it shied away from me in surprise. Soon afterwards, a mature doe stepped nervously into the open and looked behind her, hinting that she had either been disturbed or had followers still in the trees. I waited, not wanting to orphan any roe kids, and sure enough a young roe followed her into the open. Drawing a bead up the young roe's front leg I settled the reticle on the heart and lung area and released a 100-grain Norma soft-point. The positive thud of a bullet striking home saw the follower burst into a death sprint. I reworked the bolt and swung on to the old doe that fled across the glade. She stopped before entering the trees and looked back, which proved her undoing. I halted my breath and added another roe to the tally.

*England rugby international
Paul Huntsman with his doe*

*Four of the team with
the morning's result*

Not long afterwards, Chris came onto the ride and waved his hat at me. It had been him who moved the two roe towards me. I acknowledged his wave and he disappeared around the bend with his faithful labrador Fern at heel.

I didn't have another chance at a shot that morning, but when we stopped after our first session we had an impressive bag of 11 roe. That evening we resumed the offensive in an adjacent block and took six more by the same method. The total for the weekend was 29 roe; it was 85 per cent of my required cull figure taken in just one well-planned weekend.

I must stress that an operation of this kind only works once each season, as the deer seem to become wise to it immediately, but it can be effective and is often the only option if you are well behind on numbers. The objective is to quietly move, not drive, the deer.

On the continent, specific breeds of hound have been developed to move roe to static rifles placed in high seats, and this method is used extensively for both bucks and does.

The difference is this: a short-legged scent hound sticks to the roe's route and slowly presses it to move forwards until it passes a high seat. A mobile stalker moves around the roe's territory, and his presence or scent compels the wary roe to use their escape routes and deer paths. Even one operation of this kind per season is enough to show the remaining deer the error of following these routes. The hound, on the other hand, is relentless and gives the deer no let up, forcing them to consider what is coming from behind instead of the danger that may be ahead.

You may ask why we shouldn't cast off the labrador to achieve the same thing. A labrador, or any dog with much length of leg, would move the deer too fast, forcing them to bolt in a straight line and disappear into the distance. These European purpose-bred breeds, originating from bassets, have very short legs, making them slow plodders and good speakers. Breeds such as the Drever hound and the Basset bleu de Gascogne push the roe just enough for them to make a figure of eight around their territory, and are ideal for this purpose.

Needless to say, safety considerations are paramount in an operation such as this. Static rifles must be briefed about no-shoot areas, the route taken by the stalking rifle and any possible emergence points near their position. Both the stalking rifle and his accompanying dog should wear some blaze orange to make them readily visible. With correct planning this is a very efficient way to catch up on cull numbers and has pulled me out of the mire on a number of occasions in the past. **PC**

GENERATION GAME

The youngsters of today will, of course, be the future of our sport tomorrow. Our heritage will hopefully – indeed, will have to – live on through them, and never before has this been more important. Modern thinking and the associated biased schooling that goes with it makes stalking, and other live quarry shooting, sound very uncool to many of today's youngsters. Plus the readily available myriad of alternatives to fieldsports will certainly tempt many away, towards other, more 'politically correct' pastimes.

But what can we do? We cannot force our children into what we follow as a way of life. We can guide them as best we see fit, but ultimately it will be their choice to take up fieldsports or not. The negativity towards fieldsports in modern schooling is a formidable thought. At private schools it is less so, but even then there is often significant prejudice against fieldsports. In recent years the RSPB even stooped low enough to target young, impressionable children with an online game called Raptor Mountain, which despicably depicts gamekeepers as poisoning persecutors of our country's birds of prey.

At a young age, Sienna shows a stalker's instinct

Thankfully the so-called charity took the game down after the uproar it caused. But this doesn't stop them from shamelessly impressing on any who will listen that the gamekeeping profession is made up of criminals. The answer is to set aside the time to explain the rights and dispel the wrongs that almost every child will have to deal with at some point in their formative years, and encourage wherever possible any interest shown in following family tradition into the field. The continuation of our sport depends on it, and all of us should take time out from our busy schedules to encourage and guide any interest displayed by our children, or indeed other youngsters, willing to take part.

I was asked by a landowner of one of the estates where I manage the deer to take his daughter out stalking, as she was currently studying estate management and wanted some practical stalking experience. Henrietta was delightful company, and she thoroughly enjoyed two outings on her father's estate. She experienced a stalk into a roe doe to observe her at close quarters for quite some time before she skipped away, and later saw a successful conclusion and gralloch after an opportune shot by me on a suitable cull buck.

Photo: Shutterstock

What was very interesting was the open mind that Henrietta displayed at all times, and the relevant questions she asked throughout. Although this young lady had been brought up in a large estate environment, she still very much considered the morality of shooting deer and the justification of doing so. And despite having a good grasp of woodland

*The right kit ensured it
was an enjoyable stalk*

*Sienna has truly
caught the stalking bug*

management, she clearly wanted to understand all angles. Thankfully, I think I pointed out the ethical validation of culling deer in a rational way, and I left her with a couple of good books to help with her studies. The experience was a real privilege for me to get the right message across, and I have no doubt that Henrietta will go on to successfully manage her estate, or indeed someone else's in the future, and possibly even take up stalking herself.

I feel that all of us inherently harbour something of the hunter-gatherer spirit from our forefathers. I remember well my grandfather taking me out waterhen's egging as a small child, harvesting the first clutch and leaving the second to hatch off. It was the same with lapwings' eggs, or 'turfits' as they were then known locally. He showed me how to snare conies, and safely steered me in the proficient use of his old Belgian-made .410 shotgun.

I used to listen wide-eyed to the old sergeant major's stories of his exploits hunting leopard in the Sudan or fighting the Fuzzy Wuzzies with fixed bayonets. His brother was a local gamekeeper who fell in the first war, and his father, my great grandfather, was a vermin catcher, who made his living as a warrener. After surviving the same war that had claimed two of his other sons, he was cruelly killed when out rabbiting as the spade he was using to dig out a stuck ferret was struck by lightning.

The point is a simple one: the hunting seed had already been sown long before in my DNA, it had been nurtured in my formative years and steadily grew to fruition as I reached adulthood (which took quite some time in my parents' and teachers' eyes). My twin brother certainly has it, though to a lesser degree, and my sister had it too as she used to ride to hounds and occasionally still stalks. But even without such a suitable upbringing into fieldsports, the hunting gene is still there in all of us.

My granddaughter has shown a natural interest in following me into the field. Two years ago she enjoyed a number of successful evenings observing me duck flighting, and even accompanied me and gamekeeping scribe Tony Megson out on the Humber Estuary wildfowling. Mindful that early experiences are seared into a child's memory, I ensured a hot water bottle inserted into the front of her jacket and a couple of pocket handwarmers would keep the bitter cold at bay. After shooting a number of duck on the creek, we stopped shooting and watched the whistling duck come in. At one point there must have been a dozen cock wigeon just yards away from the hide, their 'weow' whistles echoing out hauntingly across the moonlit marsh. This was an experience that will live with her for a lifetime.

Last year I felt it right to take her out stalking, and so it was on the opening morning of the buck season 2013 we headed off into the wind with high hopes of grassing a buck. Sienna is always keen to do her bit and be involved, so I consciously passed her the stalking sticks to carry, and made her very much part of the team effort.

Stopping often, deliberately glassing the hedges and pointing out likely-looking areas, I made everything as interesting as possible – not that there was any need, going by the regular tugs on my jacket and the subsequent barrage of whispered questions fired at me. It's worth noting that a suitable pair of quality binoculars are a good investment for encouraging a child's interest in stalking.

It wasn't long before we spotted a suitable cull buck and a mature doe feeding at one of the pheasant hoppers. Ghosting to the floor, I indicated a long belly crawl forward into some dead ground containing a pond where we would hopefully get into a suitable shooting position. The seven-year-old kept flat to the ground and belly crawled better than most clients I have guided. Her only black mark was when I stopped and carefully rose to a knee to glass the deer and make sure they were still where they should be. Sienna, frustrated by her lack of height, stood up behind me to employ her own binoculars. Glancing back to make sure she had kept up, I was horrified to see her standing in the open. A firm, corrective nudge and a glare got her to conform admirably after that.

Eventually we reached the pond and, after ensuring she had her ear protectors in place, I rose carefully on the shooting sticks and drew a bead on the buck's vitals. The shot ran true, and after a short rush the beast collapsed dead. Giving him a few minutes to be absolutely sure he had expired, I answered the next set of questions from my charge. Explaining why he had run forward a few yards after a perfect heart shot, bullet expansion, the difference between shotgun and rifle cartridges, and why we had to wait for the confused doe to move away before we approached our quarry, took some time – but her queries eventually answered, it was time to carefully inspect the fallen beast.

Approaching from behind, I tested the buck's eye response with the sticks to be absolutely sure he had left this world. I then let Sienna take it all in and examine him before I bled the beast and set about the gralloch. I could see her brain working overtime, and she soon came out with some interesting comments: "I kinda feel sorry for him, but I do understand why we shot him, and it was fun too." That'll do for me, I mused as I began the knife work.

The gralloch turned out to be an in-depth autopsy, with Sienna showing intense interest in the different organs and without showing any signs of distaste. On arrival home she was babbling away excitedly to the war office (the wife and nan respectively), reliving her first stalking experience scene by scene, after pointing out the blood on her wellies, which she considered as something of a badge of courage. The force is strong with this one, I thought, as I locked away the rifle.

If the interest is there, it just needs nurturing. Sienna has accompanied me many weekends since then, and I'm sure she will make a future stalker. If we want our sport to continue, it will be totally down to our efforts to educate and encourage the next generation. That's a grave responsibility for each and every one of us. Live for today but never lose sight of tomorrow. **PC**

Fostering young people's interest in stalking is vital for the future of the sport

ENGAGING CAPREOLUS

In the 2013 buck season season I shot one of my best ever roebucks – certainly the biggest trophy I have shot close to home. It was in June, which historically has been a poor month to tackle roe (though as I've already related, I've got something of a fondness for it). The cover is up, and the territorial instinct isn't as strong as it was in the spring. If you're unlucky, patrolling bucks almost seem half-hearted by the middle of the month. I guess as territories are established it's more a case of reinforcement against displaced roamers rather than holding and defending ground.

June or not, I take every opportunity to be out with the rifle, and on 16 June 2013 I was so glad I did. It was a hot, sunny afternoon and the cover was high – despite the late spring, by mid-June the undergrowth had caught up. At this time of year foot stalking is a slow affair if you are not to repeatedly bump bucks. They have the advantage and they know it. A buck could as easily be 20 yards away as 200, and tempting as it may be to rush on, you are better off considering the immediate ground with a careful eye. On this occasion I did just that – moving slowly, working the wind and spying every patch of briar, hemlock and under the canopy of a young plantation by dropping to one knee every 20 yards or so.

This is extremely slow work and it is so easy to become disenchanted, or become distracted and quicken the pace – I'm as guilty as anyone of that, but it is best not to let the mind wander and concentrate on what may be there. Any little patch of russet colour must be investigated with the binoculars, every little shape that resembles an antler tip or point must be scrutinised. Often as not it will turn out to be foliage or an old tree branch, but occasionally the flick of an ear or the movement of a head will give away a resting buck.

A medal-class buck secured – with granddaughter in tow, no less

And so it was as the afternoon wore on. I was slowly eating up yardage and working a substantial plantation through with my granddaughter in tow. Two people trying to work like this has its obvious disadvantages as there is twice the opportunity to be discovered. But Sienna is showing lots of promise – she is a natural stalker. Seeking out twigs and obstacles with her feet before applying full weight is second nature to her. Furthermore, she knows to stay directly behind me to avoid making two silhouettes – indeed, she is better at this than most clients I have guided.

Every so often it pays to sit comfortably and wait on the chance that a buck will move into the open. It is tempting to cover ground but at this time of the year it is better to work an area where you know a buck is present, keep the wind and seek him out, or let him come to you by taking five and setting up an ambush at a cross ride, gateway or the edge of a plantation. That's what we did on this occasion, and what came to pass was one of the most exhilarating stalking experiences for me and Sienna – one that will stay in our memories for a long time.

We took a break at the edge of a young Scots pine plantation, sat semi-hidden between the roots of an ancient oak and waited for events to unfold. Not long after, a heavily pregnant doe came by not 10 feet from us, browsing away on succulent delicacies hidden among the grass sward of the ride. Keeping still, we went unnoticed. If we had been discovered it would have been a disaster and put an end to our outing. A frightened doe bursting into flight and barking her alarm call to all and sundry would put the buck down and ruin any chance of him coming out. Thankfully she soon melted back into the trees, and I was about to move off again in the opposite direction when a distant buck barked out a challenge. There is quite a difference between an alarm bark and a challenge, and I decided to stay put.

The buck barked on a while; then he was answered by another, almost directly behind our position. It was obvious that the nearer buck was the resident – he sounded as mad as hell, grumbling between barks. The interloper, still unseen, barked on teasingly but with an air of caution. We had the wind but I knew the nearer buck would soon have us. Making the decision to move and cover a cross ride he would surely have to pass was a gamble, but one I felt was worth taking.

We moved to a good position but I felt sure the buck had at the very least sensed our presence. Thankfully the interloper still taunted him and this kept his blood up. Barking back in anger, he came on. The atmosphere was electric and I could see the amazement on young Sienna's face. Seconds went by, then I got my first sight of him. Coming on slowly with an exaggerated high-stepping movement, he moved towards us, looking for his antagonist.

I instantly assessed him as an old animal with a thick head carrying a thick, heavy rack, and raised the rifle. Running up his front leg, I touched off the trigger as the crosshairs came to bear just behind his shoulder. On report he dashed forward, but I had seen him lift and the strike sounded like a good one.

What followed was nerve-racking. He had disappeared into the undergrowth, and despite a detailed search the blood ran out. I was considering calling in a tracking dog when I almost stepped on the beast. The relief was tremendous – the shot had been good. I had secured a superb medal-class buck after what had been the most exciting engagements with a roebuck I have ever experienced. This really is what the pursuit of roe deer is all about – it doesn't get better than that. **PC**

Photo: Umberto Nicoletti

Cautious tactics pay off with a fantastic buck

FORTUITOUS JUNE

Pete puts the integral rangefinder to good use

Maintain the effort during June – it can pay off

Many stalkers regard June as a bit of an off month for hunting roebucks. Indeed, I took this view for a number of years until in 2012, by necessity and situation of circumstance, I was forced to apply extra effort after a lean spring. The results certainly changed my mind about June, and my records from that year show that, surprisingly, June was my most successful month at the bucks.

Of course, April, May and the rutting weeks in July and August will see most of the bucks harvested, with another peak in October when the bucks start to show after the post-rut slump. The spring months are when bucks are most active establishing and defending territory. Their behaviour is much more habitual, and as a consequence the stalker's efforts are better rewarded.

There is a lot of activity when the mating game comes into play during the rut, but the results are unexceptional for me. There is no doubt that it is a grand spectacle, but expertise with the call is an absolute necessity to get results. There is nothing more frustrating than seeing bucks chasing without ever offering a shot – especially when the stalker is behind on his cull target.

Indeed, sometimes even the best of callers fail to pull a buck away from his doe. I suspect it is because the doe is close to standing and the buck doesn't want to pass up on a sure thing. The trick is to apply extra effort in April and May when chance is more in your favour, and the rut will not be so important for cull targets, which will leave October in hand for any fine-tuning.

June will see buck activity tail off as territories will mostly be established. The bucks fraying and scent marking will be much reduced once May is out until a brief increase again during the rutting frenzy at the end of July. The ground cover and foliage will increase massively, and this will therefore hide much of the roebuck's remaining movements. However, despite these negatives, June isn't the time to slacken off one's efforts – a change of tactics is the way forward.

I am not the best person for high seat shooting as I am too impatient, but there is no doubt that during June strategically placed high seats will pay dividends. Sitting and waiting with the wind in your favour is, of course, pretty much the same thing, and should be employed too. The high cover certainly impedes spot-and-stalk tactics, but the bucks will still move about and ambush methods based on solid fieldcraft and knowledge of the area will reap dividends. You will know roughly what bucks you have and where they are, and time spent in the field will reveal their favoured crossing points and sunning areas.

During June, these are the places one should spend time stalking into to wait for the targeted beast. Be ready for quick target acquisition and shooting – you will have had time to assess the ambush area for a suitable backstop and no-shoot zones. It will entail lots of waiting, and the action will be brief. There will be little of the heightened excitement one experiences in early spring when spotting and stalking, but for me it is always great to be out in the field enjoying the freedom and brief respite from a heavy workload.

Of course, hard-pressed professional deer managers will treat June like any other month and apply the same effort that their job demands through the rest of the year. But to the conscientious enthusiast who by popular belief sees June as a bit of a waste of time, I implore you to maintain the effort. It will alleviate the stress later in the year if you get behind, and it will be a lot of fun too.

One thing I must stress is not to overdo it in a particular area. Spread your activities across your ground, and under no account over-stress the deer with sustained stalking in particular areas as this will have an adverse effect – possibly even making them become nocturnal.

Last June opened well for me, with a superb stalk into an opportune buck that I knew was in residence but had remained elusive. The cover was high and the wheat crop was halfway up my shins – perfect for holding dew to sodden the lower legs. I was working the wind and carefully rounding a junction of unkempt hawthorn when I picked up the movement of two roe passing into the field I was about to enter. A quick spy through the Swarovski EL Range binos confirmed a buck and a doe at 270 yards.

The approach entailed backtracking a little and squeezing under the hedge to work my way down it on the blindside, as there was very little other cover to use to my advantage. This done, I adopted a low crouching position and stealthily ate up the distance between me and the quarry. About halfway, I poked the binos through a convenient gap in the hawthorn – and my heart sank. The deer had disappeared. They had either been spooked and ran back to the wood over the boundary from whence they came, or they had lain down in the wheat crop. Despite careful glassing I couldn't pick up tips of ears or antler tips, so I feared the worst.

Nevertheless I carried on the stalk toward their last known position – and pretty much stumbled on the beasts laid up in a tramline in the security of a slight hollow that had created a small area of concealed dead ground. Luck was with me as they were facing away and still unaware of my presence. However, my movement deploying the stalking sticks – or possibly a slight eddy in the wind – alerted the pair and they stood up. Quickly fitting to the rifle, I ran the crosshairs up the buck's front leg to find the kill zone and popped a bullet through its heart. The doe, confused, looked at its fallen partner in an agitated fashion and then skipped away.

It had been a good opening to the June account – indeed, I shot half my bucks in June last year. It isn't the easiest of months to stalk roebucks, but sometimes it's certainly well worth the effort. **PC**

With an elusive buck grassed, this June stalk pays off

BEST BUCK

W e are all continually learning at this stalking game. Indeed, when we think we know it all, one of two things happens: we fail by our own inadequacies or the wisdom well dries up. No one likes a 'know it all', and it is better to have an open mind that will soak up new knowledge. "Better a listener than a teller be" is what my grandfather used to say. It was good advice, and living by the old sergeant major's ethic has kept me in good stead through the years.

Another old stalwart who taught me a lot about roe is legendary Bavarian forester Heinz Dick. A hunting guide of some renown, Heinz has guided the rich and famous from the post-war years to this day, including the famous Luftwaffe fighter ace Adolf Galland. Years ago, Heinz told me that a territorial roebuck holding ground would to some extent tolerate inferior, submissive bucks. I inwardly dismissed this as fallacy, but politely acknowledged Heinz's advice. Just recently, however, the old sage's words were proven correct.

I have become a firm convert to the use of trail cameras. They make trophy assessment and cull planning so much easier, and often tell me who's about and up to no good. I had a particular buck holding territory that covered a small, young plantation, a sizeable rape crop, a couple of wheat fields and myriad hedgerows and overgrown ditches. He was a good middle-aged buck that showed some promise, so I left him be. Interestingly, though, the camera also showed not one, but two other bucks living in the same area. I had seen the big buck chase off another male of similar stature, and he was clearly territorial by his behaviour. But he tolerated the two underlings, who the cameras showed lived apart, right through May and into June.

It wasn't only the cameras that showed their behaviour – I had observed them through the binos too. The youngsters were obviously submissive towards the master buck, but they clearly all lived very close together. Maybe one of them was his progeny, but I doubted it. A mature doe's territory overlapped that of the bucks, but she was much less tolerant of the younger males. I was keen to see how this little set-up would work out during the rut, but the cull plan said otherwise. The two underlings were shot before June's end – but at least Heinz's advice had been proved correct.

Strangely enough, after I had taken out these underlings, the remaining buck became even more territorial and began marking and fraying much more aggressively. This proved to be his downfall. When the farmer saw him make short work of a thistle stand, I got the hard word: "The buck goes or you do." I protested that the thistles were valueless. The landowner retorted, "Take a look at the damn trees." To save face, I did just that, and, though I wanted

Tasco's trail cam proved its worth

to spare this buck for a year or two, the damage being done meant the buck would have to become past tense in short order.

This proved more difficult than I had anticipated. I could have shot him on a number of occasions in the past, but now it was almost as if he had been given an advance warning. The trail cameras showed he was still resident, as did his scraping and fraying. Then one night, accompanied by the doe, he actually presented me a shot. Just as I was deploying the sticks, a heron rose noisily out of the drain below me and frightened both the deer and me. Cursing the feathered pterodactyl, I couldn't do anything more as I watched my quarry skip away to the safety of the rape crop.

Another week passed and I tried for him again. It was a fine morning with heavy dew. So fine, in fact, I was paying more attention to the other wildlife than the buck: I actually stumbled onto him. He had been couched down close by in the hedge bottom. I startled him, and he burst into flight across a wheat field and was away. Watching his flight through the Swarovskis, I saw him reach the main drain and lost him in the hawthorns.

Hoping he would stay this side of the drain, I headed into the wind with my motivation somewhat dampened. Stopping to spy some minutes later, I was rewarded with the distant sight of the buck feeding away from me on my side of the drain. This was good news. Taking the range on these superb binoculars, I saw he was 530 metres away.

I stalked in as close as I dared, and slipped out of sight down the drain bank, cautiously making my final approach. Every 50 metres I peeped over the bank to confirm his position, but at 100 metres I thought I'd lost him until I caught the gleam of his antlers. He had couched down once more. Steadily, I sneaked on to the field margin, and I was just about to deploy the stalking sticks when he stood up and looked in my direction.

I swiftly mounted the Tikka, guided the Leupold reticle up to the buck's shoulder and flicked off the safety, all in one fluid movement. One pause of breath later, the buck took the bullet in his vitals and quickly expired.

I was sad that he had had to go. I knew another would take his place, and probably do as much damage initially as this one had recently been doing. He had been a worthy adversary, and looking at his trophy in future would bring back a collection of memories about old Heinz's advice, the buck's strange behaviour, and the public relations exercise his demise had demanded. That's the thing with roe trophies – each and every one is different, and all have much greater value than a mere measurement of one's success. It's the associated memories that really matter. **PC**

The Swarovskis reveal the buck darting away...

...but Pete catches up with it in the end

JOHN JOHNSON: A DIFFERENT APPROACH

Deer manager, technological expert and businessman of many years, John Johnson has been at the forefront of the trail camera revolution in the UK. Having championed their use since before they shot to popularity, he understands their utility in assessing deer populations, tracking particular bucks and proving or disproving theories about local wildlife populations.

His long-term use of these devices has given him a comprehensive, almost personal knowledge of deer, in particular roe. He understands the pressures on roe deer in an increasingly connected, built-up world. Not for him a rushed, minimally-thought-out deer cull; John espouses the virtues of a holistic deer management system, taking into account factors as varied as population levels, gender and age distribution, habitat structure and availability of browse, co-operation with other stalkers, and data gleaned from previous culls.

He has put forward his views on camera surveys and deer management in the sporting press, where his articles are hard-hitting and widely read. He has also put his principles into practice on many estates, with the resulting benefits clear to see.

John is not one to accept the prevailing wisdom on roe management – he creates his own wisdom through research, experience and hard work. For that, he deserves to be read by every amateur stalker and professional deer manager.

MANAGEMENT OR PREDATION?

Proper deer management involves planning and calculation before you shoot. Photo: Brian Phipps

Ⅰ expect if we were all asked why we stalk, most of us would say we were 'managing' deer. If we add to this the amount of bad press that deer are getting by destroying the natural environment, and the fact there are far too many deer, then we have a licence to go out and just keep pulling the trigger with a clear conscience that we are assisting in conserving the countryside for the benefit of all.

But are we actually managing our deer or just predating them? The word management infers that there is some kind of plan, and some form of monitoring that confirms just how successfully or otherwise the plan is performing. I was surprised to hear from a landowner at a deer-oriented meeting in east Sussex that he estimated that the fallow deer population's doe-buck ratio on his property was 20 to one, and yet he was still being encouraged to shoot as many deer as possible as there were 'too many deer'. So let's ask ourselves the question: Are we really managing deer?

There are four cornerstones of deer management:
- Population, monitoring and management;
- Habitat management;
- Stalker management;
- Infrastructure management.

Photo: Andy Lee

As individuals, we can easily relate to the first two categories. With either of these we need indicators that show just how much impact our efforts are making on the population. Let's look at a typical scenario.

We have been told by a landowner that he is concerned about the amount of impact the deer are having on a specific piece of woodland following the recent publicity. So what do we do first – get kitted up and start shooting? If it is management, then we first need to assess just what impact, if any, the deer are having. We can do this by doing some initial basic surveys, looking at browse lines and general browsing impact. Key indicators in deciduous woodland environment would include bramble, ivy, honeysuckle, rose, hawthorn, sloe and other young deciduous trees and shrubs, including coppice shoots. Of course it is critical to determine just what is responsible for the browsing activity and differentiate principally between deer, rabbits and hares. Deer always seem to get the blame as they are the most visible culprit.

Monitoring the impact is comparatively easy. Deer exclosures can be created in sample areas of a woodland. They can be constructed using various types of netting. A roll of weld mess can be used to create three self-supporting exclosures by cutting the roll into three equal lengths and forming circles. If it is necessary to allow smaller mammals in the area, the whole thing can be raised six inches or so above the ground to allow rabbits in – so deer-rabbit impact can be observed as a whole, or just deer impact.

It is not necessary to use anything other than weld mesh 1.2 metres wide owing to the comparatively small area. Larger areas can be constructed cheaply using the various types of plastic deer-proof fencing that can be found on the market. As these areas will be larger it is advisable to use 1.8-metre material. Using these methods we have a simple, visible indication of the level of impact the deer are having.

Next we need to look at the structure of the population. In an ideal balanced wild population we would typically expect roughly a 1:1 male-female relationship. In herd species this ratio would be comprised of varying age groups.

There are some individuals who think more does mean more bucks, hence more trophies to hang on the wall. This is simply not true as an out-of-control doe population may well lead to loss of good habitat that in turn leads to lower body weights and a reduction in fertility.

Getting a true picture of the overall structure of the population is critical for the cull planning process. This type of data can be collected during the stalking outing, annual census or using camera trap technology that is collecting data 24/7.

While collecting this data we must take into consideration the home ranges of the various species. Roe have a comparatively small home range while the larger species can have far ranging and seasonal home ranges. In this case individual stalkers should be taking into consideration their neighbours' management activities when viewing the overall picture. Cooperation on a wide scale is critical in managing and maintaining the larger species correctly, and achieving a well-balanced and healthy population.

Lastly we need to look at the information that can be gathered from our previous culling activities. Information needs to include carcase weights, sex, estimated age (don't get bogged down in the details – yearling, middle age and old will do), in milk or not, number of foetuses and sex if possible. This information will assist in forward planning as it directly allows us to assess the health, fertility and therefore the prospective reproduction rate of the population.

So before pulling the trigger, if we are to be considered as managing the population we must be assessing, planning, carrying out the plan and monitoring on an ongoing basis, making annual adjustments to maintain the optimum level for the specific areas under management. Of course we have to consider that one area's optimum deer population may be totally different from another's, but the management process will still be the same. ▮

Managing a herd is a long-term and multi-faceted process.
Photo: Matt Smith

A clean kill of the right animal will help others thrive.
Photo: Brian Phipps

CANDID CAMERA

Trail cameras can reveal roe trophy quality

In the USA, cameras are used to identify crop-raiding creatures

So we've established that trail cams, or 'camera traps', can be used by stalkers or anyone who wants to see what is going on in a particular location for 24 hours seven days a week. For instance, they can help if we want to know whether the tell-tale scrape at the bottom of a frayed hazel sapling is the work of a buck of a lifetime or a suitable cull buck that would be perfect for the freezer.

Trail cams have been used in the USA for some years, and have brought about a whole new way to enjoy stalking. There are three main types of these devices. At the top of the tree is the professional device used by scientists on projects. These are often custom-built and based on expensive digital SLR cameras. If you want a no-hassle piece of equipment that will just do the job, then the solution is one of the mass-produced pieces of kit – freely available in the US and with limited availability in the UK. The cost varies from under £100 to well over £400.

When choosing the camera you need to consider four things: trigger time; the range of the infrared sensor; battery life; and after-dark illumination. Trigger time is how long it takes to record the first picture once the infrared sensor has registered the presence of a possible animal in range. It's no good having a set-up that takes three seconds or more to get a picture when the possible target has moved out of camera shot. Three seconds does not seem a long time, but if you study a sequence of three consecutive shots you may be surprised how much can happen in five or six seconds. Study the sequence of photographs of the buck shown here. In the time the camera has taken to trigger the first shot, the buck has reached the hazel sapling. In the subsequent two shots the buck has moved closer and is scent marking. The camera resets itself and is ready to take the next sequence within one minute, though by this time the buck has moved on. This sequence was captured using a ScoutGuard 550, which has a trigger time of around 1.5 seconds. I would suggest that it is best to ignore any trail cam with a trigger time in excess of two seconds.

The range of the infrared sensor and the width of the area within which it can detect movement are also important. The average is 30 to 40ft, with only the most expensive cameras reaching 50ft. Third is battery life. The first trail cam I purchased – for around £80 – had a battery life of a week, which I considered pretty poor. I like a battery to last for a couple of weeks minimum.

The last aspect to consider is after-dark illumination. This falls into two categories: incandescent flash or infrared. A camera with infrared capabilities will automatically switch into this mode when the daylight drops below the necessary amount. Cameras that can switch between still pictures and video mode will generally only have infrared lighting capabilities. The majority of infrared cameras operate within the visible range. That means the human eye can detect the glow of the emitters if in the direct eyeline of the unit. Most trail cams have a resolution of three megapixels, and some even have five and above. But don't be disappointed when the results of a three or five megapixel camera don't show anywhere near the clarity or depth of picture of a normal digital camera. This is due to a combination of the lens and image capture technology used in the mass-produced trail cams.

Once you have chosen your equipment, where you site it is critical. Like with any other camera, placing and lighting is the way to get the best shots. Do not place it directly at the rising or setting sun. If you do, the picture of your animal will be at best over-exposed and at worst a complete whiteout. Position the camera at waist height to avoid perfect close-ups of rabbits! Once placed, leave the area undisturbed for at least a week. Do not be tempted to revisit and disturb the site. When you do return, make the visit as short as possible. All the pictures are captured to a standard SD-format memory card, so just carry a spare card and do a quick change. If you have the luxury of more than one camera it should be possible to track movement and analyse movement patterns. In the case of a specific roebuck this should be comparatively easy; for groups of fallow deer it will be slightly more difficult. It will make the task easier if you study either individual still sequences or even short video clips. Take note of the groups' composition. If the fallow deer in your area vary in colour, note the different individuals in the groups. Not only will you get a better idea of how and when deer move through, it will also help you get to know how many may be present.

Once you have got the equipment and seen the results, you may still want the same quality of beautiful high-resolution pictures taken using a modern digital camera, but without the cost of the professional pieces of kit. This is a little more technically involved, and I wouldn't be doing anyone any favours by trying to explain the entire process here. However, if this is something you would be interested in doing, there is an option: the Homebrew. These are assembled from parts sourced in the US and combined with a modified digital camera. The main component in this type of set-up is the digital camera, plus a ready-built control board and a suitable weatherproof case. Various suppliers in the US can provide all of the necessary bits, and then it just takes some fine handiwork and delicate soldering skills to hack the camera – that is, switch its photo capabilities with a superior system. You can find much more detailed instructions, as well as all the retailers needed, on the internet. But beware: a hack that goes wrong may leave you with a totally destroyed digital camera. Once you have seen the images included here, though, taken by Tim Walter with his homebrew camera, you may think the risk worthwhile. ■

Tim Walter gets something special on camera

The USA led the way with trail cams – but the UK is catching up

Cameras can also identify diseased deer

BAITING THE LENS

Trail cameras have become an indispensable accessory

A camera trap survey is arguably one of the most powerful deer population monitoring tools you can use that doesn't require the assistance of a professional wildlife biologist or scientist. On your own, you can estimate deer density, sex ratio, buck age structure, fawn recruitment and more information that will guide you in achieving better management of the deer on the areas you manage and stalk.

There are two techniques used when carrying out a survey, baited and un-baited. This article covers the fundamentals of a baited survey. A typical baited scenario camera trap survey involves the use of one camera per 100 acres over evenly spaced, baited sites for 14 days. The accuracy of your results depends on how well you run the survey.

I have included a step-by-step guide based on the original research conducted in 1997 by Harry Jacobson and James Kroll, and simplified by biologists in the USA who conducted similar surveys. Even with this guide, you will still have a lot of questions as you work your way through your first camera trap survey. It is impossible to explain everything in a short article on a subject that has been developed over several years.

To answer those questions, the Quality Deer Management Association in the USA has published a book, Deer Cameras: The Science of Scouting, which includes four chapters devoted to helping the reader run successful camera trap surveys. If you are serious about monitoring and improving the local deer population through good management, I strongly recommend that you incorporate camera trap surveys into your population monitoring plans. This, of course, doesn't replace the other records that are kept by any good deer manager.

It must be stressed that this type of survey uses a bait to attract the deer into range of the cameras. There is no justification for using bait as an attractant to cull deer and this is classed as an illegal act.

Once the camera trap survey has been undertaken and you have your numbers, you will have an estimate of the deer population that has been separated into bucks, does and fawns. Use these data to produce estimated deer density, buck to doe ratio and fawn to doe ratio. Sort unique bucks by estimated age to evaluate age structure.

Repeat the survey annually or as regularly as possible, using the same method, timing and camera sites, allowing you to monitor trends in herd characteristics.

This may sound more difficult than it really is, but it's important to think through the details before you launch a camera trap survey, or your results may be compromised. The truth is, camera trap surveys are fun, and they can produce valuable information even for your hunting strategies. ∎

Set your camera trap and leave it for 14 days

Implementing a baited camera trap survey

Conduct camera trap surveys in pre-season (after antlers are completely grown) or post-season (as soon as the season ends but before antler casting begins). Avoid timing a survey when natural food sources are common – such as a heavy acorn crop with fallow – as this will compete with your bait. In general, maize is the best bait to use, or mineral supplement blocks if they work well on your ground. The timing is critical as antlered bucks provide the key information in the final calculation.

Determine the number of cameras needed. On properties smaller than 1,000 acres, use one camera per 100 or fewer acres. On larger properties, use one camera per 160 or fewer acres. Note: If you can't afford or borrow enough cameras, rotate the cameras you have across the survey sites until each site has been monitored on 10 to 14 days. If you do this, be sure to start the cameras at the same sites at the same time each year and rotate to new sites in the same order each year to keep survey results comparable across years.

Using a map or aerial photo of your area, mark off a grid that divides it into one block per camera needed. Select a camera site close to the center of each block based on ease of access and deer activity. Identify each grid with a number or letter (placing a numbered or lettered sign at each site so that it will appear in the photos will help you later to organise images and data by location).

Clear ground level debris at each camera site to allow for clean images of deer. Orient the camera facing north to avoid backlighting caused by sunrise or sunset.

Locate the camera approximately 12 to 20 feet from the bait, with the bait in the centre of the image. This setup may vary with the make and model of camera.

Set the delay, between triggers, for no less than five minutes to keep the number of images manageable. There is a pre-programmed "Feed" mode setting on Reconyx cameras.

Once each site is ready, "pre-bait" it for between seven and 10 days. Turn cameras on during this phase and monitor photos to ensure the cameras are working, camera set-up is good and they are capturing good quality images.

After seven to 10 days, if the deer are responding to your bait and the traffic at each site is strong, begin the next phase: the active survey.

Maintain the survey phase for 10 to 14 days. In research, 14 days captured 90 per cent of all unique deer and 10 days captured 85 per cent of unique deer.

With the size and availability of high-capacity data cards, it should not be necessary to visit the camera during the survey period. Wear gloves when handling the camera to to reduce the possibility of leaving your scent on it.

Collect cameras and compile images. Count the total number of bucks, does and fawns. "Fawns" are all deer under a year old, including button bucks. "Total" counts include known repeats of individual deer. Do not count deer you cannot identify as a buck, doe or fawn.

Study photos closely to count unique bucks based on recognisable antler or body characteristics. For example, you may have 100 total buck images but only 10 unique bucks in total. Your ratio of unique bucks to total bucks is therefore one in 10, or 10 per cent (0.10).

Multiply your ratio of unique-to-total bucks by the total of does and fawns to come up with an estimate of unique doe and fawn numbers. For example, if you have 200 total images of does and multiply it by your 0.10 ratio, you get an estimate of 20 unique does.

Apply a correction factor to your estimates. If you ran the survey phase for the full 14 days, multiply each of your buck, doe and fawn estimates by 1.11 to adjust for deer you may not have photographed. If you ran the survey phase for 10 days, multiply by a correction factor of 1.18. The results are your adjusted estimates.

A CUNNING PLOT

Photo:
Shutterstock

Habitat management is just
as crucial as shooting deer

During the past few years, there has been a swell of information telling us that there are too many wild deer, and they are playing havoc with the environment. This may be true in certain areas, but not all, and neither does it apply to all species. The species causing most concern in some areas is the fallow deer. Muntjac is also a common culprit, with the damage it causes to the shrub layer in woodlands reducing biodiversity. But the humble roe is not immune from accusations.

I believe it's time we look positively at what deer do for the environment, and take a more holistic approach to managing them. Hunters in the USA have been doing this for many years. Their activities may not all be viewed as correct, as planting food plots may be construed as baiting an area or artificially feeding a population to raise deer densities. However, planting food plots has been used successfully in Europe to produce a diversionary food source that encourage deer away from more sensitive areas.

More recently in the USA, there has been a growing interest in managing the existing habitat to benefit deer – not necessarily to increase numbers but to increase quality. Research has shown that a deer population can have a beneficial impact on their habitat by increasing biodiversity in the area. So the question is: How can we best improve the quality of our deer while improving habitats for other wildlife?

Roe deer, in particular, benefit from increased quantity and quality of browse. I noticed this for a few years following the storm in 1987, which effectively cleared large areas of woodland in the south-east. The resultant clear areas produced large amounts of new growth ideal for roe deer. Population increased, as did quality. However, an increase in population didn't actually increase damage levels because there was more suitable habitat for the deer.

If we look at the general state of woodlands in the UK, I think it's fair to say that there are large unmanaged areas that have proved too expensive to maintain for landowners. Woodland rides become enclosed and the tree canopy closes, reducing summertime light levels to the woodland floor. With the owner's permission, this can be easily remedied by increasing the width of a ride with a scalloped edge.

The width of the scallop depends on the height of the ride-side trees. A rule of thumb for the width calculation is: for ride-side trees that are 15 metres high, the minimum width of the ride would be 24 metres with a length of 50 metres, when in an east-west orientation. These areas can be alternated along the length of the ride.

If there is any roe-friendly flora, such as hazel, that has not been cut in recent years, it can be cut just above ground level and will re-grow to provide quality browse that the roe will relish in early spring – providing, of course, that there is not a huge population of fallow deer in the area that will visit regularly and prevent regeneration. Light browsing from roe may not lead to perfectly straight beanpoles, but it will mean that there is a good source of food, plus great habitat for butterflies and other wildlife.

Woodland rides with an east-west orientation gather more light than rides that run north-to-south, so concentrate on the latter where possible. The scalloped edge of these rides provides wind shelter for deer and other fauna, as well as stalking opportunities when approaching these glades.

If there are no suitable rides, look at the general structure of the woodland. There may be parts that have areas of mature hardwood, like oak and beech, which provide high protein feed as the deer enter autumn. These hardwoods may be interspersed with other species, such as birch, ash and hazel, that add to the canopy cover.

Chicory provides ideal forage for deer

A variety of seed mixes are available

Again, if there is hazel present it will provide much-needed feed for the roe in springtime. Removing these lesser species – birch for instance – will allow more sunlight to reach the woodland floor, encouraging regeneration of the ground and shrub layers, and provide areas where deer can be seen more easily.

Outside the woodland habitat, we may be lucky enough to have small open areas that can be improved for the benefit of wildlife. Our continental cousins have been doing this for many years, improving small rough grassland areas to create habitat that provides for not only deer, but also bees and butterflies. Seed mixes are available from various game cover seed suppliers, such as Kings, which has developed products using extensive knowledge of the use of such products in Europe.

If you are considering taking on any type of habitat management, firstly discuss it with the owner of the property, and then check with your local Forestry Commission advisor. There may well be woodland grants available that you can take advantage of.

We live in a shrinking world with more and more stalking pressure on deer – in particular, our premier lowland species, the roe. We need to work together with our neighbours and cooperate with management plans. The rifle is the last tool in deer management, and there is more to management than pulling the trigger. ▐▌

DEER DOGS: THOMAS MÜLLER AND RUDI VAN KETS

The European tradition of using hounds to follow up wounded game can trace its roots back for centuries. But it's more relevant today than it ever has been. Deer are more populous, urban areas more sprawling, and cars and roads more encroaching on natural space than ever before. That means it's vitally important to follow up a deer that has run on, both to ensure the creature is dispatched with minimal suffering, and to minimise the possibility of a road traffic accident.

Ancient European scent hounds have developed into the tracking breeds we know today, including the Bavarian mountain hound, Hanoverian hound and German wire-haired pointer. Although the use of deer dogs is growing rapidly in the UK, there's no doubt we are still some way behind our continental cousins, so it's no surprise we typically turn to European breeds to get the job done.

The development of a good tracking dog is no easy process. It involves careful selection of breed and pup, training from an early age, reinforcement and lots of hard work. Rudi van Kets and Thomas Müller have both dedicated their lives to the science of deer dog development. Here, their collected wisdom is included, on what to do from the very first day right through to blooding your hound in the field.

INTRODUCTION TO TRAINING METHODS

Traditionally all scent hounds in Germany and Austria were trained according to the old Hanoverian Schooling, a method where you solely used natural tracks of red deer or wild boar – no roe deer, though, as the scent is too attractive for the hound – to train the youngster. In Hanover the scent hounds were left in their kennels for almost two years without any contact with game, fresh venison or blood, just being fed with bread and thinned milk. The Hanoverian professional hunters thought they had to keep the young hounds away from any exciting experiences because it would spoil them and make them too hasty when tracking.

After World War One the Hanoverian schooling was changed, and the young hounds were now brought in contact with the game they had to work with at a much earlier stage, usually at about six months old. Nowadays the puppies will be shown a large variety of game that they might have to track in the future as soon as they can walk. The training starts at the age of about six to seven months.

The trainer will go out and watch for red deer or wild boar moving around in areas where there isn't too much high grass or dense vegetation. He will try to pick a single animal and make notes on where it walks for as long as possible. After about three hours – that is roughly the time the body scent takes to vanish – the young hound will have to work the tracks themselves on the leash. The tracker will follow on as far away as he is able to monitor the pupil. Then the hound is taken away from the track with a special command, so he will eventually realise that the handler took him off a track he has worked on purpose, not by accident.

This training will continue with an increasing degree of difficulty until the hound is following the tracks slowly and in a concentrated manner over longer periods

*Deer dog
'training shoes'*

*Laying a blood trail using the
sponge-on-a-stick method*

of time. Then the trainer can start tracking animals with lung shots, as they will definitely find these, giving the young hound a positive experience.

This method has the advantage of being the most realistic way of training. However, it is often difficult to implement. The terrain has to suit your wishes, the deer will have to be there, and the trainer able to observe over distance. Furthermore, you have to have absolute confidence in the route the game has taken, so the young hound will learn to follow the track of the animal he has been put on without changing to other tracks.

The other way of training a scent hound is by using artificial scent trails. When starting training, most trackers will drag a piece of lung or rumen and produce a drag trail. I use this easy method of training quite often, especially when I want to train the hound's stamina. It is easy to drag some piece of rumen with a long bamboo stick next to my own track for a few kilometres, wait for a couple of hours and work the trail with the hound. The disadvantage is the large amount of scent particles the hound will find on the trail.

Therefore, in the mid-18th century German foresters and professional hunters developed a method of making an artificial blood trail using game blood and putting it on the ground at intervals between one and two metres. I use a small piece of sponge, 2cm by 2cm in size, fixed to a thin stick with a nail or screw, and apply small amounts of blood from an open can or jar on the ground. I prefer this method when I have shot a deer whose blood is either coagulated or mixed with contents of the intestines.

I often have to lay tracks in difficult or very steep terrain. Having to use an open can for the blood has sometimes left me without any blood to continue the trail because I tripped or slipped and spilled the whole lot. Now I prefer to use filtered blood, which will fit in a small plastic bottle with a hole in the lid. I can put single drops on the ground and lay my trail even in very steep terrain without the fear of spilling much.

When the training starts I use about a quarter of a litre of blood for 300 metres. My experienced hound will work artificial blood trails laid with half a litre of blood some 2,000 to 2,500 metres long. The less blood you use, the better. The blood can be taken from the shot animals by using a big syringe, then transferring it into small plastic bottles. I always keep some bottles in my deep freezer.

However, my favourite way of training both my young hounds and my experienced hounds is by using the scent shoe. This shoe was been invented in the late 19th century, and was initially a split wooden plate that attached to a boot like crampons. The deer cleaves were attached to them by cutting them short and squeezing them between the two halves.

At present, several different types of scent shoe are on the market and they are all much better than the old wooden shoe. I used them a lot in my youth, and while walking on flat ground they were ok, but as soon as you had to lay trails in the hill country or the mountains, they became dangerous because you tripped and slipped permanently. New models are either made of aluminium, soft but durable rubber or steel with claws to prevent slipping.

The attachment of the shoe to your boot and the attachment of the cleaves are both extremely important. Both have to be very secure and easy to operate. When I lay a trail I start with red deer cleaves and a little bit of blood from the same animal. I put a few drops of blood from a bottle on the ground, scratch the ground with my shoes, then step into some of the blood and walk in my desired direction. This gives my young apprentice a better chance of following the trail.

This method has several advantages in my opinion. Cleaves are easy to procure and can be frozen as well. I have a large, deep freezer at home where I keep blood, cleaves and skulls of deer I have shot, which I then put at the end of an artificial trail. This is an important point. I always use blood, cleaves and either the whole deer or at least the skull from the same animal. The young hound will identify all of these as being from the same prey. This will teach him to stay on the trail I put him on.

When laying trails you will have to mark them so you will be able to verify where the hound is going. You can use clothes pegs, but I prefer coloured paper tape that I can tie onto trees or grass. Use a colour you can actually see – I choose bright blue, because even yellow or red are colours that occur everywhere. And it is imperative for you to control the young hound and to be sure he is on the trail.

It is sometimes difficult to choose a certain method of laying artificial trails. Some specialists prefer to train by the Hanoverian Schooling. I use all methods, depending on the opportunities that arise. When I see a single stag early in the morning, walking where I can see him for some distance, I will definitely take the opportunity to follow him up. Out of season I work regularly with the scent shoe. Sometimes when I have the feeling my hounds need to do a long trail, I just drag something for a few kilometres.

Be inventive but never ask too much of your hound. It is still an animal, and just like us has some good and some bad days. Take this into consideration and you will have a great companion that will serve you well for many years. **TM**

There are many ways to teach a hound the basics

Training sessions must always end in success for the young hound

HOUND DECISION

The work of a dog should be seen from two angles: before and after the shot. Before the shot, a dog is used to show the game to the hunter by either pointing or hunting freely in the drive (a tactic mainly used for wild boar on the continent). After the shot, the dog needs to find the game and locate or retrieve it. All animals, including vermin, should be searched for with a dog. Ethical practice in the field does not end with killing your quarry cleanly – you must also to try to recover it quickly.

A trained dog should be available to track. The gun is responsible for his shot, and he needs to know what happened, be able to tell others, and accompany the search. Excuses like 'no time' are not acceptable. Searching for wounded game is an integral part of the day.

A great many breeds can be used for tracking. Alpenbrack, basset hound, beagle, Bavarian mountain hound, dachshund, German wirehair, German terrier, German short hair, English setter, Griffon, Hanoverian scent hound, Irish setter, Kopov, Labrador, Munsterlander, spaniel, viszla, Weimaraner – the list goes on. In fact, the FCI, the international Federation of Kennel Clubs, recognises even more breeds.

The one condition for the use of a dog of any of these breeds is that the dog has passed a test. Each and every breed can track, but some individual dogs lack the ability to properly use their nose, some do not have a keen desire, and some are not sharp enough. The test is vital to distinguish the dogs that can track from those that can't.

There are some breeds that have been bred especially to track: the Bavarian mountain hound and the Hanoverian scent hound. Because of their careful breeding, these can be seen as specialists. But other breeds – Dachshunds, Beagles and German Wirehairs among others – have tracking as an obligatory part of their continental tests. As I said, not every individual dog has an aptitude. Other breeds, especially the German wirehairs, can do excellent work, as shown in many trials and in the field.

The size of the dog is not important. Smaller dogs are closer to the ground, and with experience they work in a more slow, concentrated manner, and produce excellent results. Quiet concentration is the ideal in a tracking hound. A dog that races down the track is unusable – it will miss too many marks.

Smaller dogs are, as experience shows, more able to stop wounded game, as it seems to be less frightened of it. But a dog's size can make it more affected by terrain. Heavy snow or thick cover do not make it easy for a small dog to stop a deer with a shot leg.

What is also important is the condition of the dog, and what we do with it apart from tracking. It is always important to look at the various breeds during

Look for a pup that is well-built, keen and attentive

tests and to decide which breed would be most suitable for the terrain where it will do most of its work. If you have a lot of hoofed game on your terrain, a scent hound should be high on the list, but do not exclude other breeds.

In conclusion: not every dog is suitable for every shoot. The important thing is what you want to do with your dog.

So which breed is right for you? This is a decision that should not be taken in one night, but only after mature reflection. You should not select a dog because of what it looks like, but because it is suitable for your way of hunting. So select a breed that can do what you desire. That is the first criterion.

Ask yourself the following questions: What will the hound be able to do? Have I sufficient opportunities to use its abilities? Can I use it in the surrounding hunting areas? Do I have enough time for it? Am I prepared to follow a course? All these questions should help you decide. But be prepared to spend a lot of time on it. I speak from experience – before I got my first scent hound I spent nine months getting the right information. All my deliberations contributed to me obtaining a Hanoverian scent hound. I have not regretted it.

So my advice is: Consider carefully. No rushed decisions – a dog is an investment that will take a lot of your time before you get anywhere near doing a real search with it. And it is you and you alone who decides on the breed that best suits you. Nobody can take your place. But you can ease the decision by obtaining information from people or organisations that specialise in different breeds.

Play it safe. Go for a dog with a recognised pedigree. It shows that the breeder has made an effort to get good dogs and is thus most likely a member of a breed society with strict rules for breeding and training.

So now you have made your choice and asked the breeder for a pup. A keen breeder will keep you up to date and transmit as much information as possible to you, so when you make a choice at 4-5 weeks old you'll have already an impression of which pup will suit you best. There are many stories about choosing a pup. I don't pay them much attention – I aim for a dog or bitch that is strongly built, keen and attentive.

Finally he or she is almost yours. It only remains to fix the collection date and to prepare for its arrival at home. Kennel ready, appropriate food, but more importantly, everybody in the house ready to receive this small pup with open arms. From now on you will experience lots of excitement and learn how a scent hound should be trained. We will also experience that perfection one day could lead to a disaster the next. An exciting story awaits us. RVK

Choose your breed based on the kind of hunting you do

Go for a dog with a recognised pedigree

INSTILLED BASICS

Some pups are naturally inclined to track.
Photos above: Alison Montgomery
Photo below: Pete Carr

Training the puppy actually starts at the breeder's kennel at about six weeks. I breed Styrian rough-haired mountain hounds and start with a piece of lung or intestine, dragging it for a few metres in a straight line somewhere in my garden, next to the kennel. At the end of the 'trail' I leave the lung and let the puppies out into the garden.

It is interesting to see how some of them will immediately find the fresh trail and follow it to the end. Conversely, some puppies will run around excited but will not able, or interested enough, to locate the scent source. Others will find the trail but are still too excited to follow it for any distance.

This is where I start selecting hounds as blood tracking specialists. The thorough and concentrated tracker at this early stage is the one I prefer for training as a scent hound specialist. A puppy with its nose down constantly, that doesn't hear or see anything outside of its task and seems to live by its nose alone, is the one I usually choose. When buying a puppy, ask you breeder how the little hounds behave. Better still, watch the pups yourself, preferably working a simple drag trail, and try to choose the young hound accordingly.

A scent hound does not need to obey too many different commands, but it should be a reliable and obedient companion when tracking and stalking. The basics must be instilled: sit, stay, heel and recall. Thereafter it is mainly a case of harnessing the hound's natural ability to track and reinforcing the basics. My hounds will progress to walking at heel with and without the leash for longer periods. They will learn to stop without any command, progressing to stopping automatically when I observe something. Furthermore, they will have to sit and stay at my rucksack for extended periods of time when I give them the command to do so. All of this is reinforcement of the basics instilled from an early stage. It is imperative to achieve this before progressing training any further.

Another important factor is the clearness of oral and hand commands. Often both are combined. Indeed hand signals are a progression of oral commands and will eventually replace the spoken commands when the hound is older and further advanced in its training.

Because I live in an area where we have red deer, roe deer, chamois and wild boar, I will not specialise my young hound to track only a single species. As a puppy and ever after, the youngster will get into contact with all of these species and the hound must be familiar with the scent and shape of its expected

quarry. It could be disconcerting for a young dog fresh in the field to suddenly find itself opposite a large stag or a big boar when all it has seen so far is just a roe doe.

Equally, I use every opportunity to get the youngster into contact with all sorts of other animals that are not quarry species. We have horses and goats at home, and cows and sheep right next door. All these animals we might some day encounter when tracking wounded game. It should be natural for the hound to stay on its track even with a herd of cows or a bunch of horses following it through curiosity. Long walks and frequent visits to stables and barns will get the trainee hound accustomed to these animals and save problems in later life that may prove fatal or expensive.

I once had a friend of mine helping me track a wounded red deer stag. When his hound was loosed to chase a wounded stag that lifted from its wound bed in front of us, things went badly wrong. The track ended with the hound abandoning the stag and chasing a herd of young heifers. The farmer was very upset about the whole affair. When I talked to my friend afterwards, he explained his hound had never had contact with farm animals before.

The same applies to game birds like pheasants, geese and hares. Get the hound used to the scent and what they look like at an early stage, but discourage any attempt to chase them or show any interest in them at all. That will make life much easier for you, and your rate of successful 'follow-ups' will rise a lot.

If you want to specialise a hound to track a certain species, it is important to imprint this species on it from an early age. Show it all the other animals and game species you might encounter that are not quarry, and make it clear with negative conditioning that they should be passed by. But take every opportunity to instil positive conditioning with the species of your choice. Show the young hound the carcases, and feed parts of them to the hound. Any interest shown in other species should be instantly smothered and discouraged immediately, either by a sharp command or a tug on the leash.

That, of course, is one of the reasons why our young trainee hound will have to stay on the leash a lot. Roaming around freely will give the hound opportunity to find all sorts of different and very interesting things, such as fresh tracks, droppings or animals to chase. This uncontrolled action will make your job of training a calm and reliable companion much more difficult, so it is always better to be one step ahead and avoid scenarios that may undo all our good work as best we can. I understand that it is easier sometimes just to let the little bugger go. But time spent at this early stage is always well spent, because you will soon have a much easier job and a more reliable hound in the end.

There is one other part of training your young scent hound that should not be forgotten. Tracking wounded animals can be a challenging job, especially when you

Photo: Alison Montgomery

Get the hound working trails from an early age

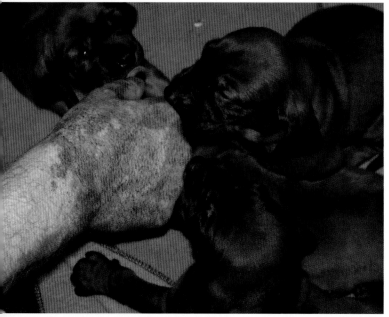

Feeding the pups with blood on your hands will introduce them to the scent
Photo: Alison Montgomery

Take every opportunity to show the hound shot game

track wild boar or red deer in difficult terrain. Following your scent hound for long hours, often bent over, trying to avoid being hit by branches or brambles, descending into gullies and climbing out of them, crossing marshes or following your hound on the chase, might bring some trackers to their knees. I stay in shape with cross-country skiing and snow shoe hiking during the winter season, and hiking and horse-riding the rest of the year. Swimming and mountain biking are also on my training programme.

Most tracker dog handlers do some sort of physical training, either while at work or in their free time. You must be able to follow your scent hound at all times, no matter what the terrain, the vegetation or the weather – in short, you must be fit. The same applies to your scent hound. I have my hounds with me most of the time when working, but I still give them some additional training when the season starts. They have to accompany me on my long hikes in the mountains, forests and marshes, the long patrol rides I do on horseback, and – the most severe, in my opinion – following me on skis or snow shoes for long hours in deep snow.

During the summer period I train them with the mountain bike and I get them to swim over longer distances at every possible opportunity. But remember, a young scent hound should not be pushed too hard at the beginning. The training level should rise gradually, just as it should for you. A puppy of 10 weeks old should not do more than one or two hours of fast hiking a day.

After teething, the scent hound's fitness and track training can be gradually increased – but only when it is fully grown at two to three years, depending on the breed, should a full training programme be fulfilled. This means your scent hound should be able to follow a track for six or seven hours on a hot and dry day and still be able to make a chase and keep a deer at bay or even pull it down for stronger types.

These are high goals, but for me this is often daily routine. Depending on your time and physical shape you may say this is way too much for you. No problem, but be sure you only start on follow-ups that you and your hound will be physically able to bring to a successful end. If you have a young, unproven scent hound, or feel the track may be too demanding, it is better to let another enthusiast with more experience take the track rather than jeopardise a follow-up right from the start. Your hound's time will come, but being fit enough to follow it through will give you the greatest chance of making the most of what will be a lifetime partnership. **TM**

TACK REQUIRED

When tracking wounded deer or wild boar, it is important to use the right equipment. Depending on the weather and the terrain, the handler's clothing choices can vary. When tracking wild boar I usually prefer thorn-proof waxed cotton jackets and trousers, because a wild boar search usually ends somewhere in dense bush, bramble or black thorn thickets. Anything less durable would end up being ripped to pieces very quickly, as would your skin.

When tracking deer or chamois in the alpine region, I prefer light and durable stretch fabric clothing, like the type worn by lumberjacks. Layering clothes, depending on the temperature, enables you to strip off a layer or two before you start perspiring too much. This is important to prevent you from getting wet, and hence chilled. Starting off shivering slightly is usually the best way of staying comfortable and healthy while tracking.

The same principle applies to the cap you wear. Ideally, it should have a visor and fit fairly tightly, so you won't lose it when crawling through thick bush. However, I personally prefer the old grey mountain cap worn by the mountain troops and forest rangers in Germany. It protects you well, can be worn in summer and winter and I hardly ever lose it. Some of my colleagues even wear climbing helmets with a chin strap, but personally I find them too noisy.

Heavy-duty leather gloves are very important – with or without insulation, depending on the weather. They will protect you from cuts when entering bramble fields or black thorn thickets. I advise you to buy them large so you can get rid of them with the flick of your hand when you have to reach for your rifle to take a shot.

Depending on where you hunt and what the legal situation is, I advise wearing clothing in blaze orange or another signal colour. Too many deadly accidents have happened because the handler was trying to approach the hound at bay or the wounded animal and was shot by another hunter eager to help, because he wasn't clearly visible. If tracking or controlling tracks close to public roads, especially when the light is fading, I also advise reflective material sewn onto your jacket. Signal vests and jackets of the type used by cyclists, or indeed anyone dealing with traffic, are also becoming relatively easy to get hold of for a reasonable price.

For your scent hound partner, you will need a special scent hound collar with a swivel leash attachment. These collars are usually two to three inches wide, and some have additional padding, but most important is the swivel attachment. This ensures your leash won't get twisted all the time and can run freely on the ground. They can be made of leather or a synthetic material, as long as they do not put too much pressure on the hound's neck and the leash can be secured safely to it – without the danger of holding the leash and the hound taking off with the collar because some rivets broke on the attachment.

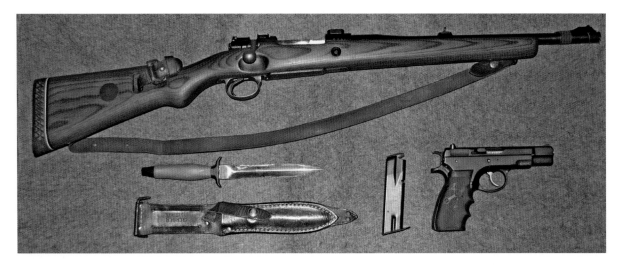

*Equipment for humane
dispatch once the deer is found*

*Reflective clothing
is a safety essential*

For the past five years I have used a chest harness to release the pressure on the hound's neck and keep the throat free to allow it to breathe properly. If you let the hound loose to chase wounded game, the collar or the harness should be taken off to prevent the hound being hooked up by a branch. This can make him hard to find if you do not use a recovery collar, or if the hound doesn't speak.

The leash should be between 30 and 36 feet long. Traditionally, a 1 to 1.5in wide leather leash is used, but in the alpine region I come from, a waxed climbing rope tends to be favoured. Leather has to be dried after its use and kept supple with saddle soap or leather oil, which is why most people around here use modern climbing ropes with a snap hook attached, or a rubberised synthetic material leash as I now use. The bright orange colour helps you to see it in high grass. They are a low-maintenance tool that has been field tested for years, and I can highly recommend them. Most important is to use a leash appropriate to your hound's size.

If your hound has been sent to chase a wounded animal, it is good to use a signal collar, or even better, a signal vest with additional reflective material and your phone number and the hound's name on it. If strangers pick it up, they can easily inform you where the hound can be retrieved.

Scent hound handlers now use hound radio retrieving collars. However, all the hounds mentioned in this series will usually find their way home sooner or later. My hounds have stayed away for up to four days, way up in the Alps when chasing a chamois up a steep cliff and there was no way to come back on the same route. They eventually waited for me where I originally let them loose, sitting on an old overcoat I left there. If you want to retrieve a lost hound quickly, I advise you to buy a radio or GPS retrieving collar, but make sure it works in your area and type of terrain (watch out for deep ravines and the like).

When coming up to wounded game you will have to decide on how to kill the animal. Usually, it is more humane to keep your distance and give the *coup de grâce* with your rifle or a powerful handgun. That said, there are situations when the use of a firearm is not advisable.

When dispatching an animal next to a road, with spectators – not to mention the danger of a ricocheting bullet – you will have to use a good hunting or military knife with a blade of five inches or longer. It has to have a sturdy blade and a proper sheath securing the knife properly, yet that allows quick access when needed. It is best worn on a belt above your jacket.

The same applies for your handgun, if you decide to use one. Most professional trackers in Germany use a pistol or revolver only as a backup gun. The calibre should be the biggest one you can comfortably handle, so you will still hit something when under pressure. Usually 9mm Para, .45 ACP in pistols and 3.57 Mag or .44 Mag in revolvers with four-inch barrels or longer will be sufficient. Use high-quality hollow-point ammunition to ensure enough stopping power.

My personal advice would be to leave the handgun at home if you are not confident in your proficiency with it. It is a lot of dead weight to toss around, and much more dangerous in a tight situation than a short rifle.

I prefer to carry a shortened bolt-action rifle in a medium calibre with a fairly heavy bullet, like my old Mauser 98 in 9.3x62. Using a heavy round-nose bullet I can shoot through thick bush as well – but good stopping power is most important. The barrel can be cut down to 18in, but the front sling attachment should be mounted as close to the muzzle as possible to prevent it from getting hooked in branches when carrying it over your back. The sling should be attached to the side of the rifle – I find that this way it is more comfortable to carry. The sling used should be strong and checked regularly for any weak spots.

A good old Lee Enfield in .303 or Mauser 98 in 8x57 or .308 Win will do the job perfectly. The rifle has to be reliable, with a well functioning safety catch that secures the firing pin rather than the trigger. I prefer to put one up the spout only when I believe I will need the rifle soon. Detachable magazines must be avoided, or at the very least secured properly; there is nothing worse than trying to cycle a round in the chamber, to find out that you have lost your magazine. As an alternative, lever action rifles like the Marlin Guide Gun or pump guns with slugs can be a good choice.

Lastly, if looking for blood or hair that the hound is interested in, a pocket magnifying glass and white tissue paper (to dab the area) can be quite useful.

When the weather is hot and dry, or you expect a long 'follow up', always take a canteen along to ensure that both hound and you will be supplied with enough water. The same applies to energy bars – following wounded game requires good kit, a keen hound, and a tenacious tracker. It can entail hours of hard work, but a successful find is more than worth it. **TM**

What you need: A selection of Thomas's deer tracking equipment

An orange leash helps you follow the hound in cover

SIGN AND SPOOR

Here, a bullet clearly hit and exited the tree

Before starting a search with a tracking hound, it is imperative to establish that the hound handler is in charge of the whole search until either he decides to quit, or the animal has been found and killed. Nobody else should give orders, and the only person finishing the wounded animal at bay should be the hound handler.

I always ask a number of questions when a hunter calls me to track a wounded animal. This is quite a sensitive topic, so be supportive when questioning the hunter. A good scent hound handler is a person of trust and integrity. Be respectful and above all reliable.

Questions one should ask include:
- Was the rifle sighted in correctly, i.e. was a test shot fired
- Calibre and ammunition used
- Confirmation of what species was shot at
- What was the shooter's position and approximate range
- Where did the animal stand
- Which side of the animal or which part was probably hit
- How did the animal react to the shot
- Weather conditions at the time

Boar hair: A clean cut shows a bullet was responsible

The information you gather will help plan the search. Then the tracker should adhere to the following rules:
- Remain calm at all times
- Memorise an animal's position and posture when shot
- Mark the shooting position with an indicator
- Wait at least 15 minutes before you look at the shot strike area (unless there is danger of losing sign – such as in falling snow, etc.)
- Never let loose any dog directly after a shot!
- If you cannot find any sign call a more experienced scent hound handler
- Never disturb the area where the animal was initially shot at

The next step will be going to or establishing the shot strike area. Only the hunter who actually fired the shot should accompany you here, to avoid disturbing the area. If he or she is carrying a gun, insist it is unloaded. If the shot strike area can be located, drop your hound 20 to 30 metres and look for sign alone. Decide if or where the bullet has actually hit the animal. Look for a bullet mark in a tree or on the ground, cut hair, blood, skin, bones, teeth, flesh, gut content, hoof or antler parts and anything else to help build a picture of the hit and what to expect. Shot animals usually dig in their hooves and rip the ground when fleeing.

If you cannot find the exact strike area, take the hound on the long leash and let it search for any signs and spoor. Keep the leash fairly short so you can see what the hound shows you. Allow for wind drift when finding hair. Start around the strike area and work in circles going wider and wider to find either the shot strike area or the track of the animal.

If you find lung blood – a light pinkish colour and frothy – the animal is usually found within 200 metres, depending on the bullet and species shot. Start tracking after half an hour – this is enough time for the animal to die calmly. Any other signs, such as liver blood or pieces of bone, require at least three hours' wait.

Wounded animals tend to hide and wait to see if they are being followed up. The animal will soon stiffen and be less inclined to run if left a while. Disturb them too early and most will run on until they drop, resulting in a long and difficult chase.

Assess the shot strike area.
Look for a blood trail

I prefer tracking alone. If I am not familiar with the terrain and the area, I will permit a local guide to accompany me, but he should be physically fit enough to follow me without any stops. I have lost too many 'guides" especially when the animal was just ahead, the hound was slipped and I had to run to keep up.

There are some general rules as to how animals might react when they have been struck by a bullet, but remember these are just indications and not gospel. The same applies to different types of blood, hair and bones found. If the hunter was able to see through the recoil, he might have noticed how the deer jumped off. If hit high close to the vertebrae, an animal usually drops on the spot, but might get up and run away after kicking violently – a sure sign the vertebrae have been hit or shocked.

The same can happen when throat shot or the antlers have been hit. Head shots missing the brain will see animals shake their heads when bolting. There may be saliva, teeth and pieces of bone. A shot through the lungs will produce light-coloured, frothy blood with some short hair from the flanks of the animal.

Liver shots show dark brown blood, most often with pieces of liver tissue in it. The best way to confirm liver blood is to taste it. Liver or gut shot animals hunch up at the shot and walk or run off with their backs raised.

If you are not sure of the blood indication, rub it between your fingers to see if it is just blood. A shot through a muscle may show some fibres when rubbing it between the fingers, a stomach or intestinal shot may smell and be bitter to taste.

The best way to learn is by examining shot animals thoroughly. Look at the different types of hair from different parts of the body, colour, and length in seasonal pelage. Try to memorise the hair, shape and layout of bone structure, colour of the organs and the blood coming from them. The best way to memorise this is by preparing lots of animals for the table.

If no signs have been found, this does not necessarily mean you have missed the animal. Follow the track for at least 400 metres, and if you haven't found any sign then quit the search. Never quit too early, though – there is nothing more disappointing than calling it a day only for the dead animal to be found days later. This has happened to most professional trackers – due diligence always applies. **TM**

HARE OF THE DOG

Scent shoes can serve a purpose, but hounds will tire of artificial tracks

Using hares is a tried and tested training method

Training specialist scent hounds is really a variation of two different methods. Most hunters will opt for the artificially laid trail method, mainly for its relative ease of use and certainty of the trial direction, which is made increasingly difficult as one goes on. Using less and less blood over a longer trail and the inclusion of scent shoes using deer or wild boar cleaves will create as natural a looking trail as possible for the hound. However, never underestimate the dog's abilities – he will know that this isn't the real thing, but he will get the idea of what you want him to do.

The trick here is to keep him occupied and always make it fun for the hound, the minute he loses interest suspend the activity, and always endeavour to make the hound succeed and achieve its reward. Do not overdo the tracker training – basic training should always be reinforced as part of the young hound's growing up process. This will form the foundations of recovering wounded game, and produce a well-trained, obedient hound to be proud of.

Once every two weeks is enough for artificial scent trail training, and there's definitely no need to do it more than once a week. But if the second method of training using the old Hanoverian way of schooling is used, this can be done more often. This method is only limited by one's ability to find a suitable stag and both watch and mark its progress to be later followed up by the hound in training – not an easy task, as I am sure you will agree.

A variation of the Hanoverian method that I use involves using the humble hare as an alternative tracking subject. I understand this suggestion may cause a collective breakdown among British hound handlers as the hare is often considered anathema to any sort of gundog training, but please, hear me out.

In my area, individual hares are much easier to locate and observe than the elusive red deer stags. Therefore I have adapted the training of my young hounds to include hare hunting as well as stags. In operation it is simplicity itself, as the hares are quite easy to locate and I watch closely their chosen path across the fields before introducing the young hound to its trail at a point of my choice with the necessary command.

I must make mention of the obvious here: avoid substituting rabbits for hares. All tracking hounds must be broken of their natural inclination to chase rabbits – there is no benefit to a hound tracking a short distance to a burrow. The hare, however, will cover its area over lesser and greater distances, with the added advantage that it won't take refuge under ground.

In reality the hare's track is a difficult one to follow and loses its scent very quickly, which concentrates the hound's mind and nose, effectively conditioning the hound to focus on the scent and forsake all others. I work hare tracks just like any other trail, and the training effect is absolutely great. When the hound has flushed the hare, I will let him chase it for a while, as a reward. This really cements the training to follow a single track and is always fun for the hound – they will never tire of the real thing, unlike artificial scent trails. German and Austrian houndsmen actually have a saying that a good hare chaser – or 'courser' to use the British parlance – will always become a good scent hound. In my experience, this is absolutely true.

I must again stress the fact that basic training must always be instilled into the young hound so the handler can effectively harness its natural hunting ability. The hound must be steadily conditioned to work for you and not for itself. Ultimately the handler will be able to call the hound off a hot trail if it makes a mistake and it must only be allowed to hunt trails of the handler's choice. Of course when the hound is fully trained and experienced it will often be let off for long periods to hunt a trail on its own, but although it will be tracking free, it will be tracking a scent it was instructed to by the handler. This is worlds apart from a hound rioting off any interesting scent it likes.

Keep your hound on the correct scent

So please do not dismiss the humble hare as a way of using the Hanoverian method of schooling, the handler can always break the hound off hares at a later stage of training, and indeed using artificial scents across areas frequented by hares is a great away way of conditioning the hound to hunt hares where commanded. Over time, all will fall into place, just don't forget that some hounds will learn faster than others.

Expanding on this theme with a hound that has properly instilled basics, which has also shown promise on artificial tracks, the next step would be to lay a trail in a deer park. Getting permission may not be that easy, but look for a deer park manager with a tracking hound and you may be successful.

This is a sure way to teach the hound that it must stay on the line instructed by you, despite the more interesting scents around it. Again do not over-do the artificial scent training and always be inventive and make it as interesting as possible for the hound.

A combination of the above methods is what I have used successfully, and I have no doubt that they will be as successful in the UK, too, if adapted by forward thinking handlers who have confidence in their charges. **TM**

The end result: An obedient hound that works well

CALLING IN BACK-UP

Identify the right time to call in the deer dog

The correct behaviour of a hunter consists not in firing a shot alone but also in their behaviour towards the game, including searching for it and gralloching it correctly. I believe every hunter has to keep certain standards towards nature in general and game in particular. Every hunter who has wounded deer or boar has a duty to do his utmost to recover it and stop its suffering.

In practice this means he has a moral duty to call in a specialised tracking dog. This all comes from the hunter's behaviour before and after the shot. If we shoot, we aim to kill the animal as quickly as possible. We do everything in our power, with precise guns, the right ammunition and a good scope. But occasionally we notice that the opposite occurs. The results are badly wounded game.

Before we shoot, we must observe the game, its behaviour, how it appeared, and so forth. These factors will make us decide whether to shoot or not. If we place a bad shot then the above will be of importance when we start tracking as it might determine if the wounded animal goes into cover or flees. Hence the benefit of observation.

We must carefully observe the various reactions of the shot game, starting with the sound of the bullet strike. It is useful to have heard this before as some of us do not hear it at all while others hear it too well. After we shoot, reload immediately as it is quite often the case that when the game is not killed outright it gives us the chance for a second shot. Often I ask the question: Why didn't you take a second shot? You get a variety of answers.

Assess the shot location and reports of the animal's behaviour

I did not want to damage the game; I did not think about it. With large animals it may be a good idea to give a second shot. Once the animal is on the ground, we give it the famous five cigarette minutes.

We now have the opportunity to verify our thoughts – shot, reaction, location, and direction of flight. Did the animal indicate it was wounded? Try to recall it all. A wounded animal's reactions can vary enormously. Many factors play a role. I am not a ballistic expert, but in general one can say the greater the calibre, the bigger the wound. This makes it easier to track with our hound.

The law prescribes certain calibres for certain types of game and there are, of course, many different bullets in the same calibre. One can generally state that an animal shot with a .375 will be easier to track than one with a .243. We often hear the argument that a smaller calibre does less damage to the carcase. That is true, but we have an obligation to the animal to let it suffer as little as possible and to kill it cleanly.

We have to make a serious calibre choice. I recommend a minimum of 8mm for red deer, sika and wild boar, and 7mm for the other species. Of course, a big stag in the rut can be cleanly killed with a .243 if the bullet is correctly placed, but better a bigger calibre. It is not easy to collect evidence of all shot types, but that could be helpful to our investigation of the shot place before we start tracking.

To go into a little more detail, the quantity of blood lost will depend not only on the bullet type and size but also on where it hit the body (high or low). The higher the shot, the less blood.

It is our aim for the game to go into the nearest cover and stay there. Therefore, we leave it in peace. After five or 10 minutes, we go quietly to the shot place. We can now investigate it and find what evidence is available. Be careful – loud talking or calling might cause the wounded game to flee further into the cover with all the consequences that entails.

The wounded game may well be close to the shot location. We have to consider whether the game still has signs of life and give it a bullet. We go back to the shot place and walk the first few metres of the track. Do not walk on the track itself. If we do that, we might destroy important tracking elements that are important later for our hound. The most common mistake is that the hunter immediately follows the track, disturbing the game, which flees further into the cover. Searching with a torch in darkness is also to be avoided and can be seriously dangerous if one searches for a wounded boar. Many a continental hunter has bad memories from this.

With certain wounds, blood will not show until further down the track

After the shot, be silent. The wounded game will go into a wound bed and quite often stay there. We find no signs on the shot place and imagine the game is missed. Now we will do a control search with an experienced hound. If we think we missed and cannot find any shot signs, it is quite often that we find the bullet strike.

We also have a picture of the situation until now. Sometimes we can draw the conclusion that we missed. Occasionally, when the animal we shot at is part of a group, we can look at its behaviour. Did it join the group running away or did it go in a different direction? In the latter case, we always complete a thorough search. Missed or not. RVK

READING THE SIGNS

The type of blood can tell you a lot about the shot

U sing the guide here, accompanied by the easy-reference table, we can interpret a variety of shot signs to better assess the significance of the hunter's shot. We should start with the premise that the location of the shot, the bullet strike, and the impact site of the bullet will result in different reactions from the animal. The aim of the shot is to destroy the nervous system; this can lead to many diverse responses. We must also take into account the exact point of impact, the condition of the animal, and the type of bullet used. If we presume that we have used the right bullet then we will concentrate on the animals' reactions – meaning the behaviour of the animal as it is shot. This behaviour and the nature of the bullet's impact will be our starting points. From here, we can start the recovery.

SHOT REACTIONS

Let's start with the classic heart shot. In reaction to this, the animal will jump, collapse or run away. We can often differentiate between high and low heart shots; with a high heart shot the lungs will be hit and the search for the animal will be longer.

If the shot goes just behind the heart, there will be no clear signs – but if the bullet is further back, it's a stomach shot. In this case, the animal will kick with its hind legs and retreat quickly into its wound bed. The liver will have been penetrated, and fatal blood loss will force the animal to cover.

If shot in the liver, the animal bends its back and runs a few hundred metres. By observing the flight we can see whether the animal is severely wounded.

A kidney shot causes one of the most distinctive: The animal will collapse and cry in pain, but will get up again. Observe carefully – the hind legs might be paralysed. If so, be patient – it will die in its wound bed within two to four hours.

Let's move on to the less common (and less lethal) shot placements, typically only taking place in error. If a shot touches the spine, the animal will collapse, then kick with its legs, get up and run away. Try another shot, otherwise it will be very difficult to recover it.

If the bullet hits its leg, the animal will limp on the hit leg and run; in this case, all you are likely to find is bone fragments. The animal gets used to these wounds, so it will seldom go to a wound bed, meaning a difficult search lies ahead. If the leg shot was particularly high, a vein may rupture, presenting more vivid red blood.

With no clear signs, the hardest shot to interpret is probably the jaw shot. Worse, it is very difficult to recover a jaw-shot deer. Additionally, the animal will suffer for days after being shot, before eventually dying of starvation. You will commonly find teeth, tongue, blood and whatever was in its mouth at the shot place.

Watching the deer's reaction is key

If no vital parts are hit (a 'meat shot'), the animal won't show signs – it will simply run away. Blood will mostly be vivid red, which diminishes further along the track. This quarry is more recoverable in the winter.

Finally, a mere superficial wound – a bullet strike that causes shock, making the animal fall then run away. Blood loss can be heavy, but the animal won't be mortally wounded.

Bear in mind that roe and red deer show clear shot signs, but wild boar less so. It is also important to remember: animals that have already been shot at will present fewer, less obvious signs, and a rutting deer will be similarly stoical, so watch closely. Behaviour will differ depending on the surrounding area and context, and whether the shot was from a high seat. **RVK**

Pay attention to surroundings. Not all strikes are obvious

SHOT SIGNS: REFERENCE GUIDE

Heart or lung shot
Vertical jump, then the animal runs for up to 200 metres
Half-long hair found at shot place
Lung blood is vivid red and foaming

High heart shot
The animal either jumps vertically or collapses
Long hair at shot place
Lung blood is vivid red and foaming

Liver shot
The animal bends back then walks away slowly
Red-brown blood with small liver fragments
Wait for about two hours; the animal will die in wound bed

Kidney shot
The animal bends back and then goes into cover
Small amount of blood: dark to medium red
Half-long hair found at shot place
Blood mostly in droplets

Spine shot
Total collapse
Fatal shot

Stomach shot
Flees either quickly or slowly, depending on bullet placement
Small amount of blood: medium red with stomach content
Fatal but will still run a long way
Wait 4-5 hours before tracking

Gut shot
Kicks with hind legs, sometimes bends back
Medium red blood with gut content
Half-long hair found at shot place
Fatal if left alone; the animal will go into wound bed
Start tracking after 4-5 hours

Shot shocks top of spine
Falls on its back, waves its legs for a few seconds then runs away
Long hair at shot place
Little or no blood
Animal will seldom be recovered

Jaw shot
Few visible signs at first other than a shake of the head
Short hair and fragments of bone
Bright red blood with mouth mucus
Not immediately fatal. Animal must be recovered as otherwise it will starve slowly

Meat shot
Animal flees
Depending on location different sizes of hair
Medium red to bright red blood
Mostly the animal recovers if the shot is only a flesh wound

Leg shot
Animal will limp on the side of impact
Short hair, bone splinters found at shot place
The higher the shot, the greater the amount of medium-red blood
If both legs are broken the animal either remains still or moves with its hind legs
Animal can recover, not often fatal if only one leg injured

Superficial wound
Animal marks, then runs away
A lot of hair with occasional flesh found at shot place
Vivid red blood, more at the place of impact then less within a few metres
Not often fatal

BASC TROPHY MEASURING SERVICE

The British Association for Shooting and Conservation

The BASC measuring system has been operating for six years. But it is since 2012 that it has really taken off, expanding and evolving in association with *Sporting Rifle* magazine. It now measures virtually half of the trophies measured in the UK.

The BASC service has seen a steady uptake among stalkers over the years and is now seen as an important part of the data record of successful deer management in the UK. Our vision is that a partnership of the largest shooting organisation in the UK with the only magazine specifically for deer stalkers will ensure many more trophies are brought forward for measurement and recording. This will contribute greatly to the archive of deer and in particular roe management in the UK since the 1950s. It will also ensure greater publicity is given to management practices that result in the presence of premium specimens.

For many years the CIC's measurement was the European benchmark for the measurement of quarry species. To ensure consistency with historical records, the BASC system was benchmarked to the CIC criteria, but has since introduced various changes and rationalisations to make the measurement of deer antlers in the UK more accessible, more inclusive and more logical. Nevertheless, our system still tends to produce total scores that are within 1-3 per cent of CIC measurements. This is the same differentiation that is normally found between all trained and experienced measurers, whatever their backgrounds – hence the requirement for panels of measurers in some European countries. Our aim is to ensure that BASC measurements remain comparable to those offered by other systems, but also bring in many previously unrecorded trophies and provide a significant contribution to UK data and statistics.

We have also expanded our measuring team, in particular adding members located in the parts of the country known for producing premium trophies of the various species. Our aim, by having access to on-site measurers, is to include the significant proportion of trophies that are shot by foreign stalkers and taken out of the country without being measured. This will greatly

The BASC team at the Midland Game Fair

The BASC deer programme

Arran Deer Stalking scheme

enhance the records we keep. To achieve this, we are not bound by the 90-day rule but measure trophies 'fresh', and rely on the experienced experts involved to make appropriate weight deductions where heads are clearly 'wet'. This is no more than what measurers did successfully for many years before official CIC involvement. BASC measurers work rigorously to maintain quality control throughout this process.

One of the major successes of the partnership has been a new platinum award for roe and muntjac. There is such a difference between a roe head of 150 points and one of 130 that it seems inappropriate not to recognise that difference with a different award and a new medal. For roe of 150 points or more, and for muntjac of 70 points or more, BASC now awards a platinum medal, and we have seen several of these awarded in the two years since its in inception. On top of this, we redesigned all our medals to mark the start of the partnership.

As for the formulas themselves, there were some minor changes and some more significant ones. For example, there is surely no other way to assess a sika or muntjac trophy than by length of beams, span and tines. But since the measurement does not include weight, we do not insist on the 90-day rule for these trophies.

For fallow and red we have taken a different view. Weight is counted, but it amounts to typically no more than 2-4 per cent of their respective scores. So we feel it is perfectly acceptable to make an educated guess as to weight where the measurement cannot actually be taken. This means shoulder-mounted red and fallow are eligible for a measurement. The certificate will be marked as 'estimated weight'. We feel that experts in their species should have little problem assessing likely weight. We also introduced a 130 per cent rule to upper beam measurement to ensure antlers lacking a second tine can still be eligible for upper beam measurement.

Having spent several years as a CIC measurer, I am particularly interested in its roe formula. It certainly selects the correct criteria and makes the proper definition of a premium trophy, but it is not without fault. Where possible we have made changes that introduce greater logic to the definition of a trophy, but without changing the nature of the measurement, so our results are comparable to those recorded since the 1950s.

With roe, weight amounts to 30-40 per cent of the total score. It is far too important a criterion to estimate, so shoulder-mounted roe trophies are still ineligible for measurement. But 'wet' trophies can have their weight loss estimated by an expert measurer, thus abandoning the need for the 90-day rule.

We have made several other alterations to make the formula more logical. In CIC scoring, for example, span scores rise in graduations from 0 to 4 depending upon width-length ratio, but then drop from 4 to 0 rather arbitrarily, often penalising a perfectly pleasing trophy. Our system adds equal graduations from 4 back to 0. Additionally, colour is scored from a colour reference chart, and

New medal designs have been introduced

A rare three-antlered head submitted by M Hamblen

additional tine scores have been completely overhauled to avoid effectively scoring the same thing twice.

Anyone who has ever tried to measure a Chinese water deer tusk using a steel tape will be aware that the circumference can be manipulated by how hard you pull the tape. This undermines circumference measurements to the extent that they add nothing at all to a measurement. On top of that, the measurement is almost always 30mm anyway. The BASC system responds to this by measuring canine length only and reclassifying the medal award as if the circumference measurement was 30mm.

Finally, we have added the 'Yearbook entry' category for roe that fall just short of a medal but have scored over 100 points. This is clearly an excellent roe, and any heads matching this criteria are listed in *Sporting Rifle*'s reports on the trophies to come through the BASC system. This change in particular has been very well received.

Despite all these changes, the system is still very much a work in progress. Everything is continually subject to constant scrutiny and review. We want this system to be 'by stalkers for stalkers' and, to that end, if there is anyone who feels they have a particular contribution to make, I would be very pleased to hear from you. In the meantime, thank you to all those of you who have supported this programme since its inception in 2008. **DG**

Stalking stalwarts: Marco Pierre White, Peter Carr, Wes Stanton and Dominic Griffith celebrate the success of the new measuring service at the Sporting Rifle awards

BASC TROPHY SERVICE:
2011 REVIEW

2011 was an interesting year where roe were concerned. Every so often, as in 2010, you get a bumper year in terms of quality – but then, unfortunately, every so often you get a diabolical one too. And 2011 was a diabolical one. These are statistical blips, but they are of great interest to roe enthusiasts such as myself.

No one knows what causes these peaks and troughs but they are well documented. While the UK is famous for its fantastic roe, and many of us take huge satisfaction from seeing the visible benefits of sound management practices, there remains something about roe that both taunts and captivates. We used to say, for example, that you needed a hard winter for a bumper roe year. Well, we certainly had a hard winter over 2010/11. But too hard? Despite so many things appearing to remain constant (food, cover, management input) the roe still manage to confound us.

Most of the professional stalkers I talk to chose to minimise the mature buck cull of 2011 in the hope that 2012 would be better. All this meant that for the measuring service it was a quiet year in terms of roe. Just 33 medal-class roe are recorded, and only seven of gold medal quality. But that is not to detract from those few magnificent specimens.

We enjoyed another successful Game Fair with medal-quality heads of each of the six species measured. It was here that we saw N Dewing's Berkshire

Above: T Hehir's gold-medal fallow

Left: A medal head from Wiltshire – the heart of roe country

monster roe of some 170 points, which definitely proved the exception to the rule. Most of the other roe presented for measurement achieved silver medals, and I think we all felt that in a better year these might have achieved gold.

Of the other species, there was an exceptional Devon stag that achieved bronze, and L Beerden's huge Berkshire muntjac buck of 76.1 points, which I think makes it the sixth biggest ever recorded. We also saw two magnificent Dorset sika stags, which both belonged to S Adamson and achieved silver medal status. But above all there was N Griffith's Galloway red stag, which is measured as the new Scottish record.

Since then we have seen M Poffley's Berkshire roe trophy of 148.75 points, D Hunt's gnarled old Wiltshire specimen of 141.9 points and T Hehir's two magnificent Hampshire heads, together with his rare gold medal fallow. I particularly liked M Hamblen's three-antlered roe (pictured on page 150). As ever, Hampshire remains the centre of great roe, but it will only remain so if we continue to practise the highest standards of management.

Thank you to everyone who brought in their trophies for assessment. I would also like to apologise to the stalker whom I had to disappoint. He proudly showed me what had been described to him by the other organisation as a coalesced buck – but despite what he had been told, a true coalesced buck is one that grows a single antler from fused pedicles and, although often having the appearance of a normal six-pointer, actually grows and casts as a single unit.

Sadly, the buck brought in was simply one whose antlers had grown very closely together and would have been cast as two separate antlers albeit somewhat interknit. A great trophy in any event, but not a coalesced. **DG**

N Dewing with his huge roe

BASC TROPHY TABLES

E Davies 161.37

A Enggaard 160.5

X Elen 116

ROE

Platinum	Location	Score
L Mulcock	Wiltshire	187.3
E Davies	Gloucestershire	161.37
A Enggaard	Gloucestershire	160.5
Silver		
W Ashman	Wiltshire	129.5
P King	Wiltshire	121.35
W Ashman	Wiltshire	120.6
J Elen	Wiltshire	116.85
A Brunel	Hampshire	116.55
W Ashman	Wiltshire	116.4
X Elen	Wiltshire	116.0
Bronze		
H Bain	Oxfordshire	114.55
W Ashman	Wiltshire	113.55
J-P Harle	Wiltshire	113.45
S Fairbank	E Yorkshire	113.45
A Enggaard	Gloucestershire	113.2
J Elen	Hampshire	111.25
P Schwerdt	Wiltshire	110.9
Furst Lowenstein	Hampshire	110.25
S Fairbank	E Yorkshire	106.55
P King	Hampshire	105.52

MUNTJAC

Platinum	Location	Score
M Brackstone	Wiltshire	75.9
G Annawitt	Bedfordshire	70.3

CWD

Gold	Location	Score
G Williams	Bedfordshire	224.0
G Annawitt	Bedfordshire	214.0
Silver		
G Annawitt	Bedfordshire	202.0

P Osterbrink 107.1

D Clements 114.45

D Wilson 109.6

Bronze

C Arnold	Bedfordshire	188.0

JUNE 2012

ROE

Gold	Location	Score
M-P White	Hampshire 2010	137.1
M-P White	Hampshire 2010	134.3
C Willoughby	Somerset	132.2
Silver		
P Leggett	Hampshire	126.03
A May	Aberdeenshire	125.57
R Waller	Hampshire	118.15
D Clements	Hampshire	114.45
D Clements	Hampshire	112.0
Bronze		
S Pike	Somerset	110.88
D Wilson	Oxfordshire	109.6
P Osterbrink	Devon	107.1

MUNTJAC

P Leggett 126.03

D Boyes 141.05

J D Spencer 124.55

P Lavender 127.5

Gold	Location	Score
G Josey	Berkshire	66.0
R Hawker	Hampshire	62.0
Bronze		
P Leggett (RTA)	Bedfordshire	58.2
G Josey	Berkshire	57.5

JULY 2012
ROE

Platinum	Location	Score
J D Spencer	Surrey	154.5
Gold		
D Boyes	Hampshire	141.05
K Coles	Hampshire	140.15
C Willoughby	Wiltshire	134.55
Silver		
P Lavender	Hampshire	127.5
J D Spencer	W Sussex	124.55
M Heron	Dorset	122.3
A de Ryck	Belgium	119.25
G Schwarzenbach	Berkshire	117.1
Bronze		
B Rolphe	Wiltshire	113.2
A Miller-Mackay	Hampshire	107.8
P Cummins	Hampshire	105.92
Yearbook qualify		
S Coe	S Yorkshire	104.9
B Johnson	Lincolnshire	104.85
N Loft	Berkshire	103.3
P Unwin	Germany	102.95
P Schwerdt	Wiltshire	102.85
Louis(c/o Poffley)	Berkshire	102.85
J-P Vanthielt	Wiltshire	102.55
R Cawood	Yorkshire	102.37
P Schwerdt	Wiltshire	102.15

MUNTJAC

Gold	Location	Score
D Webber	Wiltshire	68.4

A Ironside 116.4

A Powell 108.9

AUGUST 2012

ROE

Gold	Location	Score
G Bass	N Yorks	138.8
M Pile	Hampshire	137.65
Silver		
A Ironside	N Yorks	116.4
Bronze		
P Schwerdt	Wiltshire	110.8
A Powell	Lincolnshire	108.9
Dr S Johanny	N Yorks	106.7
A Bennett	Hampshire	106.2
R Barnes	Hampshire	106.1
Yearbook qualify		
A Brunel	Hampshire	102.85

MUNTJAC

Gold		
M Pile	Hampshire	62.5
Silver		
P Williams	Hampshire	60.1

SEPTEMBER 2012

ROE

Gold	Location	Score
J Weir	Berkshire	138.35

R Barnes 106.1

A Bennett 106.2

H Eikelaar 113.8.jpg

S Hawker 135.3

J Weir 102.45

J Weir 138.35

S Hawker	Warwickshire	135.3
A Keane	Yorkshire	131.5
R J Hinds	Berkshire	131.1
Silver		
S Crook	N Yorkshire	128.4
T Jonson	Ayrshire	124.8
Bronze		
H Eikelaar	Berkshire	113.8
Yearbook qualify		
J Weir	Berkshire	102.45

FALLOW
Silver

L Crook	Norfolk	171.5

MUNTJAC
Gold

J Tunmore	Suffolk	61.8
Silver		
S Hawker	Warwickshire	59.6
S Crook	Norfolk	58.9
Bronze		
J Weir	Berkshire	56.0

OCTOBER 2012

ROE

Platinum	*Location*	*Score*

T Lusby 113.25

A Hall 114.75

J Smith 113.72

C Hipkin 118.55

J Kroll	Angus	150.65
Gold		
J Kroll	Angus	145.35
N Grellis	Surrey	142.27
J Carnegie	Buckinghamshire	138.0
G Campbell	Cumbria	134.25
Silver		
K Scott	Northumberland	127.95
J Hewer	Cumbria	119.3
C Hipkin	Somerset	118.55
H Nicholson	Surrey	117.35
J Stirk	Yorkshire	115.25
Bronze		
A Hall	Kent	114.75
P Stark	Yorkshire	114.7
J Smith	Warwickshire	113.72
T Lusby	Cumbria	113.25
P Jones	Suffolk	113.15
G Campbell	Cumbria	111.55
J Stirk	Yorkshire	111.05
P Jones	Suffolk	111.0
G Siddal	Devon	110.55
S Warris	Suffolk	110.3
T Lusby	Cumbria	110.2
P Woodcock	Northamptonshire	106.02
J Smith	Warwickshire	105.55
Yearbook qualify		

J Huck	Cumbria	104.17
G Siddall	Devon	102.05
D Scott	Galloway	100.8

WILD BOAR
Bronze

| R Atkinson | Germany | 111.85 |

MUNTJAC
Gold

J Carnegie	Buckinghamshire	69.3
J Renouf	Cambridgeshire	66.1
A Barrett	Bedfordshire	65.2
J Renouf	Cambridgeshire	63.9

Silver

| J Renouf | Essex | 60.4 |
| J Renouf | Cambridgeshire | 60.0 |

CWD
Gold

S Bottrill	Bedfordshire	224
S Bottrill	Bedfordshire	216
A Barrett	Bedfordshire	206

JAPANESE SIKA
Gold

| J Anderson | Lancashire | 268.1 |

NOVEMBER 2012

ROE

Platinum	*Location*	*Score*
S Penfold	Hampshire	165.15
Gold		
A May	Aberdeenshire	148.05
J Silvester (Baillie-esque)	Hampshire	146.25
N Thorpe	Hampshire	140.5
B Wallbot	Oxfordshire	136.3
T Hehir	Hayling Island	135.4
J Macnee	Hampshire	131.6

N Grellis 142.27

B Wallbot 136.3

N Thorpe 140.5

J Gill	Surrey	131.15
Silver		
T Hehir	Hampshire	124.6
R Ahearn	Hampshire	122.6
T Hehir	Hampshire	118.3
T Hehir	Hampshire	115.8
Bronze		
I Hannah	Wigtownshire	109.2

FALLOW
Bronze

A Bennett	Hampshire	161.62

MUNTJAC
Gold

J Hunt	Hertfordshire	65.1
J Hunt	Hertfordshire	63.7
D Geel	Gloucestershire	63.0
A Smith	Warwickshire	62.0
Bronze		
L Pulford	Norfolk	56.0

DECEMBER 2012
ROE

Bronze	**Location**	**Score**
A Lovel (RTA)	E Yorkshire	110.32
A Lovel	E Yorkshire	107.9
P Carr	Wiltshire	105.35
Yearbook qualify		
P Carr	E Yorkshire	100.52

CWD
Gold

C Dimitriou	Bedfordshire	217
Silver		
P Swatman	Norfolk	204

JAPANESE SIKA
Gold

T Lander	Dorset	282.5

J Silvester 146.25

P Carr 100.52

A Lovel 107.9

BASC TROPHY SERVICE:
2012 REPORT

*Steve Penfold's
Hampshire giant*

*Dominic and Paul Childerley
assess another trophy*

If I am completely honest, I never expected the new BASC and *Sporting Rifle* initiative to be quite the resounding success that it has turned out to be. In 2012 the team measured 216 trophies of all six species of deer as well as a handful of wild goats and boar. We measured trophies from 27 counties of the United Kingdom and a handful from Belgium and Germany.

We reached a total of 187 medal-class trophies, of which 113 are attributable to roe. The list of roe includes 32 gold medals, of which seven attained the new platinum level of 150 points or more, 35 silver medals and 46 bronze medals.

Medal-class roe have been recorded in 24 counties – although, as ever, 25 per cent of these emanate from Hampshire – and the inclusion of all trophies scoring 100 points gives important recognition to another 18 quality roe trophies. The platinum award proved to have been pitched at exactly the right level for both roe and muntjac, with just six roe and four muntjac attaining that rare accolade. So of the 34 medal-class muntjac trophies from 14 English counties, 23 achieved gold medal status, of which those four scored platinum. Another six silvers and five bronzes complete the tally.

The statistics demonstrate a tripling of the number measured, and a tripling of the number of recorded gold-medal roe. Inarguably this now recognises the BASC and Sporting Rifle measurement system as a database of equal and significant value to the overall UK quality register. With this system in just one year growing to account for 40 per cent of all English and Welsh recorded medal quality roe, it seems clear that stalkers are choosing a system based on credibility rather than on tradition.

It was a year with some special memories. In the spring, Lee Mulcock brought in his fantastic Wiltshire roebuck of 187.3 points, together with some great photographs of it. His decision to cull was based on years of observation, and the correct decision that it was now passing its peak.

It remained the largest roe trophy measured in the year, despite a last-minute bid from another Wiltshire monster of 171.25 found dead by Godfrey Pitman. Steve Penfold's Hampshire buck of 165.15 was particularly memorable for being his first buck, and one I very much doubt he will ever exceed.

The fact that the CLA was cancelled meant we had the busiest Midland Game Fair that I can ever remember. Most notable there were the pair of roebucks taken by Jan Kroll in Angus, of which one was a platinum of 150.65 and the other a gold of 145.35. Of the other species, Mike Robinson's Oxfordshire fallow of 189.86 and Tim Lander's Dorset Japanese sika of 282.5 stand out as exceptional.

But the service is not only about the best trophies from the prime areas. Equal recognition is given to the many heads that were presented from the less well-known areas of the UK. With reference to sika deer, I have had correspondence regarding the origin of the Bowland sika. Although they appear in skull to be Japanese, and the nasal bone measurement matches that of Japanese sika, my feeling is that based on the balance of the evidence that I have seen, we should in future measure them as Manchurian. We would welcome any further information. **DG**

Godfrey Pitman's head of a lifetime

Lee Mulcock's unforgettable trophy

C Dalton 135.5

G Burgees 113.17

G Pitman 171.25

JANUARY/FEBRUARY 2013

ROE

Platinum	Location	Score
G Pitman		
(found dead)	Wiltshire	171.25
S Vincent	Hampshire	152.05
Gold		
C Dalton	Ayrshire	135.5
Silver		
R Wyatt	Oxfordshire	126.0
F Gascoigne	Oxfordshire	122.65
H Eikelaar	Berkshire	117.8
Bronze		
J Maiden	Dorset	114.2
G Burgees	W Sussex	113.17
F Gascoigne	Oxfordshire	113.7
A Purvis	Scotland	112.7
M Beevers	Dorset	106.0
R Wyatt	Oxfordshire	105.0
Yearbook qualify		
F Highton	Hampshire	104.85
S Miller	Speyside	102.77

MUNTJAC

Silver		
T Rudd Clark	Wiltshire	59.7
Mr Abel	Bedfordshire	58.9
Bronze		
P Schwerdt	Berkshire	57.5

CWD

Gold		
C Maw	Bedfordshire	226
M Whiteford	Cambridge	216
Bronze		
C Dimitrou	Bedfordshire	182

WILD BOAR

Silver		
R H White	Turkey	115.5

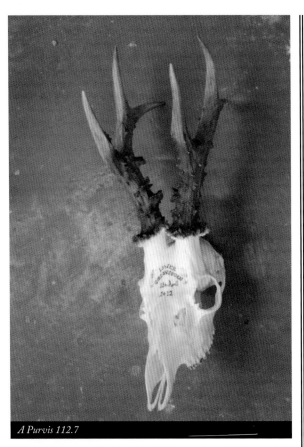

A Purvis 112.7

S Vincent 152.05

S Strawbridge 101.97

MARCH 2013

ROE

Yearbook qualify	Location	Score
S Strawbridge	Devon	101.97

FALLOW
Gold

D Watson (found dead)	Hampshire	192.47

MUNTJAC
Gold

P Fuller	Bedfordshire	65.4

J Rawson, 127.05

C Von Hobe 107.25

c/o K Coles	Wiltshire	64.0
Silver		
S Shuckford	Bedfordshire	60.4
Bronze		
J Folkard	Essex	57.2

CWD
Gold

S Crook	Cambridgeshire	222
Bronze		
S Crook	Cambridgeshire	192

APRIL 2013

ROE

Gold	*Location*	*Score*
T Barfoot	Wiltshire	132.47
Silver		
J Rawson	Hampshire	127.05
S Kirby	Kelso	117.77
Bronze		
T Lowry		
(found dead)	Hampshire	114.92
T Lowry	Wiltshire	110.0
C Von Hobe	Hampshire	107.25
T Lowry	Hampshire	106.2

FALLOW

T Barfoot 132.47

Bronze

S Rowntree	Warwickshire	165.51
R Phillips	Derbyshire	165.09

MUNTJAC
Platinum

G Spragg	Gloucestershire	70.4

Silver

T Barfoot	Wiltshire	59.6
R Star	Berkshire	59.1
S Rowntree	Bedfordshire	59.0

Bronze

W Cave	Gloucestershire	57.9
S Crook	Norfolk	57.3
S Rowntree	Bedfordshire	56.9

CWD
Gold

J Hetherington	Bedfordshire	228
J Hetherington	Bedfordshire	210

Silver

L Thornley	Bedfordshire	208

Bronze

L Thornley	Bedfordshire	182
J Hetherington	Bedfordshire	178

WILD BOAR

T Lowry 106.2

S. Kirby, 117.77

T Lowry 110.0

Silver

C Reyner	Poland	115.15

MAY 2013

ROE

Platinum	*Location*	*Score*
S Jones	Gloucestershire	166.55
c/o T Lander	Gloucestershire	162.45
Gold		
M Voigt	Hampshire	134.55
Silver		
P Watry	Hampshire	125.5
P Schwerdt	Wiltshire	118.7
P Schwerdt	Wiltshire	116.7
Dr H Oaktree	Wiltshire	115.25
Yearbook qualify		
c/o K Coles	Wiltshire	102.85
P Schwerdt	Wiltshire	102.0
P Schwerdt	Wiltshire	100.65

MUNTJAC

Gold		
T Wright	Wiltshire	68.4
Bronze		
P Watry	Hampshire	56.0

CWD

Silver		
A Smith	Bedfordshire	190
Bronze		
M Dempsey	Bedfordshire	178

JUNE 2013

ROE

Gold	*Location*	*Score*
K Whitehouse	Warwickshire	139.95
Silver		
F Lefebure	Wiltshire	122.25
T Lowry	Wiltshire	116.8
Furst Lowenstein	Hampshire	116.7

c/o T Lander 162.45

P Schwerdt 118.7

T Lander and S Jones

Bronze

A Wilson	Northumberland	110.82
K Whitehouse	Warwickshire	110.05
Count J Moy	Hampshire	108.7
J Rawson	Hampshire	105.07

Yearbook qualify

B Isambert	Berkshire	102.4
P Schwerdt	Wiltshire	100.15
B Larsen	Wiltshire	100.1

WILD GOAT
Silver

S Rowntree	N Wales	327.5

MUNTJAC
Gold

Count J Moy 108.7

T Lowry 116.8

J Rawson 105.07

W McLaughlin	Lincolnshire	68.0
P Opperman	Hampshire	61.8
Silver		
W McLaughlin	Lincolnshire	60.5
Bronze		
W McLaughlin	Lincolnshire	57.2

SIKA
Gold

J Johnson	Sussex	263.4

JULY 2013
ROE

Platinum	*Location*	*Score*
S Hill	Surrey	171.85
J Copeman	Warwickshire	167.42
A Woods	Gloucestershire	150.8
Gold		
G Turnbull	Gloucestershire	135.45
M Hunter	Scotland	135.02
G Boxall	Surrey	133.9
P Adams	Northumberland	133.7
J Clare	Cumbria	133.7
W Koen	Hampshire	133.45

F Lefebure 122.25

G Jones 122.9

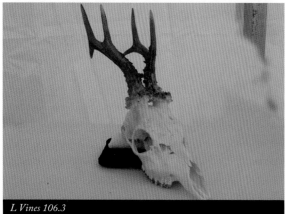

L Vines 106.3

B Hitch 130.0

A Campbell	Warwickshire	130.77
W Koen	Hampshire	130.05
B Hitch	Gloucestershire	130.0
Silver		
F Nesbitt	Northants	125.8
D Hinsley	Oxfordshire	125.75
J Hurt	Wiltshire	125.2
G Jones	Perth	122.9
D Simmons	Wiltshire	122.85
J Hurt	Oxfordshire	120.95
M Western	Gloucestershire	119.1
R Fishwick	N Yorkshire	118.4
R Williams	Cornwall	118.4
Bronze		
N Cowley	Gloucester	113.9
M Nicholson	E Yorkshire	113.4
A Carr	N Yorkshire	112.25
G Jones (found dead)	Perth	110.05
W Koen	Hampshire	109.72
W Koen	Hampshire	109.5
D Gibbs	Berkshire	109.47
J Scott	N Yorkshire	107.5
M Higgins	Northumbria	107.15
R Everett	Sussex	106.6
P Surmon	Somerset	106.5
S Duggan	Powys	106.45
L Vines	Wiltshire	106.3
G Fenwick	N Yorkshire	105.75
Yearbook qualify		
L Christoforou	Oxfordshire	104.55
J Bayles	E Yorkshire	104.55
D Gibbs	Berkshire	103.22
W Koen	Hampshire	101.4
P Harter	Powys	100.7
R Thomas	Hampshire	100.25

MUNTJAC
Gold
R Thomas	Hampshire	61.2

Silver

J Lewellyn	Bedfordshire	58.7
Bronze		
B Hitch	Gloucestershire	58.2
A Van Hoylandt	Hampshire	57.8
R White	Leicestershire	57.0
N Bracey	Gloucestershire	56.4
N Bracey	Gloucestershire	56.3

RED
Gold

Anonymous	England	199.69
Bronze		
J Allen	New Zealand	167.81

FALLOW
Gold

R Joyce	Sussex	181.72
Silver		
L Vines	Romania	175.86

WILD BOAR

| L Vines | Bavaria | 110.45 |

AUGUST 2013

ROE

Platinum	*Location*	*Score*
P Davis	Hampshire	152.2
Silver		
M P White	Found Dead	128.25
M P White	Hampshire	127.15
Bronze		
M P White	Wiltshire	114.3
B Bartlett	Aberdeenshire	112.47
A Bennett	Hampshire	105.4
Yearbook qualify		
A Bennett	Hampshire	104.05
P Davis	Hampshire	102.5
B Larsen	Wiltshire	100.1

WILD GOAT

G Jones 110.05

G Fenwick 105.75

A Carr 112.25

Silver

J Korsgaard	N Wales	337.0
J Korsgaard	N Wales	329.8
P Labram	N Wales	324.1

MUNTJAC

Gold

P Howard	Oxfordshire	67.4

SEPTEMBER 2013

ROE

Platinum

	Location	Score
M Norris	Hampshire	162.0
A Jackson	Perthshire	150.85

Gold

P Garraway	Gloucester	136.55
D Leigh	Lancashire	132.8
S Applegate	Wiltshire	131.85

Silver

H Ochtree	Wiltshire	127.5
A Willmot	Gloucester	126.85
P Garraway	Gloucester	126.85
R Waller	Hampshire	123.7
R Stapleton	Hampshire	121.25
D Applegate	Somerset	120.45
R Martini	Somerset	120.25
T Green	Lancashire	119.3
A Younger	Hampshire	118.5
M Stapleton	Hampshire	118.25
M King	Devon	118.0
D Smith	Lancashire	116.75

Bronze

R Waller	Devon	114.6
R Waller	Hampshire	112.35
J Allen	Worcestershire	111.15
D Moor	E Yorkshire	110.95
S Frost	Gloucestershire	110.2
A Langrish	Hampshire	110.1
J Sale	Somerset	105.4
T Taylor	Angus	105.2

P Davis 152.2

M P White 128.25

M P White 127.15

M King 118.0

M Stapleton 118.25

Yearbook Qualify

K Pickering	Caithness	103.7
G Adams	Cumbria	102.75
R Waller	Hampshire	102.45
D Worthington	Cumbria	102.5
J Elliott	Cumbria	102.1

MUNTJAC
Gold

E Pockett	Berkshire	63.2
T Hunter	Buckinghamshire	61.8

Silver

D Walters	Gloucestershire	59.4
S Frost	Buckinghamshire	58.5

OCTOBER 2013
ROE

Gold	Location	Score
A Pink	Hampshire	146.6
T Hehir	Hampshire	135.5
T Hehir	Hayling Island	130.15
Silver		
S Berry	Wiltshire	126.3
T Hehir	Hampshire	125.3
T Hehir	Hampshire	122.75
D Hunt	Wiltshire	117.75
Bronze		
T Randle	Hampshire	113.4
M White	Berkshire	112.7
Yearbook qualify		
K Wilp	Devon	104.6
M Hasa	Dorset	103.5

MUNTJAC
Platinum

R Hawker	Hampshire	73.3
Silver		
O Rowlands	Berkshire	60.9
Bronze		
O rowlands	Hampshire	56.0

RWaller 102.45

R Stapleton 121.25

J Elliot 102.1

CHINESE WATER DEER
Gold

N Froom	Bedfordshire	234.0

NOVEMBER/DECEMBER 2013

ROE

Gold	*Location*	*Score*
R Morgan	Gloucestershire	134.05
Bronze		
D Clements	Hampshire	112.0
J Wadge	Scotland	108.0
Yearbook Qualify		
D Hayes	Norfolk	100.43

MUNTJAC

Silver		
J Weir	Hampshire	58.5
Bronze		
D Clements	Hampshire	56.3

RED DEER

Silver		
C Reyner	Norfolk	180.08

JANUARY/FEBRUARY 2014

ROE

R Morgan 134.05

BASC TROPHY SERVICE:
2013 REPORT

The year 2013 saw further expansion and consolidation of the BASC and *Sporting Rifle* trophy measuring service. We measured a total of 251 trophies, of which 211 achieved medal classification.

The trend shows little change in recorded quality from 2012, with a broadly similar number of gold, silver and bronze roe trophies – slightly more platinums, fewer golds, a number of additional silvers, the same number of bronzes and a significant number of additional yearbook qualifiers. Of the other species, again a similar profile emerges to match 2012.

We were incredibly busy at the Ragley Hall CLA Game Fair, with a team of four working constantly from early morning until late afternoon measuring 66 trophies of the various species.

The number of heads continuing to be presented show there is no shortage of trophies – but most stalkers say it was not a fantastic year. What small factors create more or bigger golds in a particular season? It is almost certainly down to annual variations in environmental conditions of which we do not have a full understanding.

Despite this, there were many lucky stalkers who enjoyed great success, and there are a number of memorable trophies that spring to mind. Early last year, a New Forest fallow buck found dead beside the road was brought in for measurement. Measuring 192.47, it is probably the biggest wild fallow buck ever recorded. Curiously, we found, lodged in the back of its head, the .32 bullet that the dispatcher had used to end its misery. This trophy has now been set up by Andover-based taxidermist Greg Keeble.

J Copeman's Warwickshire platinum head

Of the nine platinum roe, all of which are truly outstanding trophies including those from Warwickshire, Gloucestershire and Hampshire, S Hill's Surrey buck of 171.85 is the largest and takes a place in the top 50 roe ever recorded in England. Among the gold-medal roe are examples from Cumbria, Northumberland and Lancashire – areas that have only recently begun to produce roe of that quality. The muntjac this year were a little disappointing, with only two achieving the coveted platinum award. This has much to do with the fact that most landowners see them as an invasive species that should be shot on sight. Without management input they thus rarely achieve their full potential.

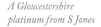

A Gloucestershire platinum from S Jones

But it is not all about the biggest trophies – it's about maximising the potential of your particular piece of ground to whatever level it can produce. So equal recognition must be given to the many bronzes and yearbook-qualifying roe that emanate from the less productive counties of England and Wales. They represent at least as great a success as producing a gold medal in Hampshire or Gloucestershire. **DG**

S Mackenzie 107.85

D Delacato 149.18

D Newton 139.37

K Doddington 110.35

Gold	*Location*	*Score*
D Delacato	Gloucestershire	149.18
D Newton	N Yorkshire	139.37
Bronze		
K Doddington	Oxfordshire	110.35
S Mackenzie	Isle of Skye	107.85

FALLOW
Bronze

P Carr	Bedfordshire	167.86
P Schwerdt	Berkshire	163.51

MUNTJAC
Gold

M Talbot	Wiltshire	67.3
S Little	Wiltshire	65.1
R Smith	Wiltshire	62.6
J Robson	Norfolk	62.1
S Little	Wiltshire	61.0

Silver

Eric (c/o M Poffley) 130.65

S Mackenzie 107.85

Louis (c/o M Poffley) 157.25

N Jewell	Hampshire	60.4
Bronze		
J Robson	Northants	57.2

CWD
Silver

J Robson	Norfolk	200.00

WILD BOAR
Gold

P Carr	Hungary	122.6
Silver		
S Palmer	Romania	116.75
Bronze		
J Robson	Bulgaria	112.2
J Robson	Croatia	110.2

MARCH 2014

ROE

Platinum	*Location*	*Score*
Louis (c/o M Poffley)	Berkshire	157.25
Gold		
Eric (c/o M Poffley)	Berkshire	130.65
Silver		
A Stalker	Dorset	122.23
Louis (c/o M Poffley)	Berkshire	118.72
Eric (c/o M Poffley)	Berkshire	116.5

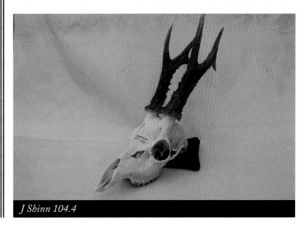

J Shinn 104.4

Eric (c/o M Poffley) 114.5

A Stalker 122.23

Bronze

Eric (c/o M Poffley)	Berkshire	114.5

Yearbook Qualify

S Mackenzie	Isle of Skye	107.85
J Shinn	Cumbria	104.4
Eric (c/o M Poffley)	Berkshire	100.2

FALLOW
Bronze

K Coles	Wiltshire	161.82

APRIL 2014

ROE

Platinum	Location	Score
K Coles (RTA)	Hampshire	154.45
M Gibson	Hampshire	151.4
Gold		
P Carr	E Yorkshire	147.0
Silver		
J-P Arley	Wiltshire	125.6
P Carr	E Yorkshire	117.67
Bronze		
S Mackenzie	Isle of Skye	107.85

K Coles 154.45

P Carr 147/0

P Carr	E Yorkshire	106.6
Yearbook Qualify		
J-P Arley	Wiltshire	103.65
P Carr	E Yorkshire	101.5

MUNTJAC
Gold

A Heard	Wiltshire	64.8
L Payne	Wiltshire	61.7

CWD
Gold

A Lake	Norfolk	218

MAY 2014
ROE

Gold	**Location**	**Score**
N Thorpe	Hampshire	135.65
N Thorpe	Hampshire	134.5
P Oldring	Hampshire	133.4
Bronze		
N Thorpe	Hampshire	112.1
N Thorpe	Hampshire	111.75
Furst Lowenstein	Hampshire	111.3
J Bustamente	Hampshire	109.15
S Parish	Devon	106.7
Count J Moy	Hampshire	105.8

J-P Arley 103.65

M Gibson 151.4

N Thorpe 112.1

ROE STALKING WITH THE EXPERTS **181**

RECOMMENDED READING

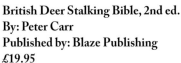

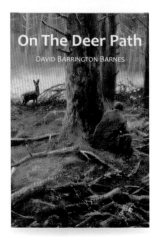

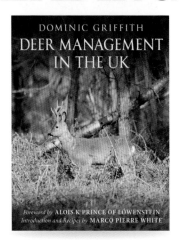

British Deer Stalking Bible, 2nd ed.
By: Peter Carr
Published by: Blaze Publishing
£19.95

The *British Deer Stalking Bible*, *Sporting Rifle* editor Pete Carr's debut book, quickly became a sell-out and an essential addition to the stalker's library. New for 2014, this second edition has been extended and modernised with updated photography, new stalking equipment, an additional hunting story, and a new preface.

On the publication of this edition, the author said: "I originally set out to record the experiences I have been fortunate enough to enjoy since I first picked up the rifle. But I soon realised many newcomers would ask questions on how to get started and what equipment is needed. So there is a significant section on rifles, optics and other necessary paraphernalia."

On the Deer Path
By: David Barrington Barnes
Published by: David Barrington Barnes
£15 (£12.75 from virtualnewsagent. com)

On The Deer Path should not be thought of as an instructional tome – it is so much more than that. Although the book starts with David grassing his first stag under his mentor's guidance in Scotland, the book is really concerned with low-ground deer, and the author's honest and often humorous account of becoming a self-taught stalker. David has done a skilful job of transferring his enthusiasm for the sport to the page.

This delightful book will definitely raise a few knowing nods and smiles of empathy from those who have trod the deer path, and it will inspire many newcomers to take the same way.

Deer Management in the UK
By Dominic Griffith
Published by Quiller
£25 (£21.50 from virtualnewsagent. com)

Dominic Griffith is without question one of the most knowledgeable stalkers in Great Britain today. A dedicated deer manager, he has been extremely generous with his hard-won knowledge, always willing to share his experience and passion for roe with his fellow enthusiasts. This book updates the author's previous records and adds three case studies of areas he has had under continuous management for 15 years. This is the first book that makes the link between theory and practice.

This book demonstrates the benefits of a gentle approach, producing an unstressed, more visible and much more manageable population of deer. It is a culmination of a working life spent with deer.

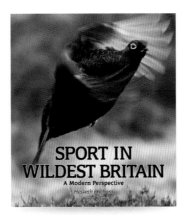

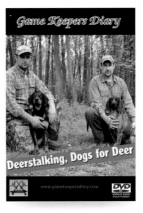

Sporting Rifles
By: Peter Carr
Published by: Blaze Publishing
£24.95

Compiled, arranged and co-authored by Peter Carr, this new book comprises a collection of modern sporting firearms available to the British centrefire rifleman, complemented by their respective calibres from the diminutive .17 Hornet all the way through to the big game calibres. It covers rifles for almost all live quarry hunting scenarios, but particularly deer stalking and fox shooting. Furthermore, this book offers a valuable, impartial view on the application of each rifle in the field from a notable expert. These include Byron Pace, Tim Pilbeam, and Mike Powell – three sporting scribes who really know their way around a rifle.

Sporting Rifles is a comprehensive, knowledgeable book, and it is as close to the definitive guide to modern hunting rifles as you're ever going to get. It deserves its place on every sporting rifleman's book shelf.

Sport In Wildest Britain
By: Hesketh Prichard and Peter Carr
Published by: Blaze Publishing
£29.95

Originally released just before Hesketh Prichard's death in 1922, *Sport in Wildest Britain* quickly sold out, as did the subsequent second edition. The book is still deemed one of the best books on sport ever written by a British sportsman.

Copies have become increasingly hard to find, and this, coupled with a chance meeting between another sporting author, Peter Carr, and Hesketh Prichard's great-grandson Charlie Jacoby, set into motion an idea that resulted in this, the third edition of *Sport in Wildest Britain*. It has a 'modern perspective' added by Peter Carr, plus four new chapters on species not covered in the original. Effectively two books in one, this new edition will set the benchmark for modern sporting writers, and is a must-have for every ethical sportsman who likes to pursue wild quarry in wild places.

Deer stalking, Dogs for Deer
DVD
Produced by Gamekeepers Diary
£25

Sporting Rifle editor Pete Carr and German professional hunter Patrick Rath have teamed up with Keepers Diary presenter Geoff Garrod to produce this easy-to-follow and informative hound training DVD. The basic continental methods shown will help the first-time hound trainer achieve a standard good enough to take his hound to the field. This DVD shows that training a blood tracking hound is not rocket science – indeed, it is easier to train a specialist blood hound than it is to train a Labrador or spaniel for game shooting work.

Experience comes with practice, and when confidence grows between hound and master a working bond will be formed for life. This informative DVD is essential for every stalker.

Want to know more?
Get more information at:
www.virtualnewsagent.com

ACKNOWLEDGEMENTS

Firstly I would like to give personal thanks to all the experts included in this book. When I took over as editor of *Sporting Rifle* magazine, Dominic Griffith was a regular mine of information on southern deer management and trophy measuring. Indeed, he is the most knowledgeable expert in his field today and the current head measurer of the BASC trophy records.

Likewise, Mark Brackstone gave me another vein of expertise to tap into. His knowledge and friendship have been of immense help during my editorship of *Sporting Rifle* magazine. I shall never forget the superb morning's roe stalking he provided for me where I grassed three bronze medals before breakfast. Both are longstanding contributors on their subject in the sporting press and Dominic is a published author in his own right. I thank them for the wealth of knowledge, and the unselfish way they have shared it with me in my role as *Sporting Rifle's* editor these past five years.

The same goes to the other experts featured in this book. David Barrington Barnes is another sporting author who has always been available at the end of the phone with sincere advice when needed. His style of writing is so engaging, and one I have striven to emulate. Chris Dalton of South Ayrshire Stalking's honest contributions, describing the ways that work for him, have been and still are immensely popular. Deer dog experts Tommy Müller and Rudi Van Kets live, breathe and dream tracking dogs. Their interest is infectious, and both are true gentlemen with a hunting ethic second to none. John Johnson is a breath of fresh air in the UK stalking scene. He looks beyond our Isles for modern equipment and techniques that might be useful to import to our way of thinking in Britain – he must be applauded for that. All the aforementioned I cannot thank enough for their writing, and support throughout various stages of my *Sporting Rifle* editorship. It has been badly needed and greatly valued. Without their collective writings this book would have been a much tougher task.

Colin Fallon, my deputy editor on *Sporting Rifle* magazine and an invaluable colleague at Blaze Publishing, was given the assignment of editing this book and putting right my faults. He has my gratitude and understanding for putting up with me during the compilation and structuring process, which went on for longer than it should. And for always delivering when I dish out the request he must by now dread: "Make it so, No. 1!" Whatever the time of day or night, he has always helped me without question to put a pressing project together, pass a magazine, or act as emergency camera – I cannot thank him enough. Matt Smith, another Blaze Publishing colleague, has worked wonders designing this book in such a short time frame; he has my gratitude for that.

To publisher Wes Stanton for supporting this project and injecting the necessary currency to achieve its completion – I am again in your debt, a position I always seem to be in. Thanks Wes.

Finally to my wife Debra for her continued support, and tolerance above and beyond the normal call of wedlock. I know if I'm not out shooting, I'm mostly writing about it. You really do deserve to sit among saints. **PC**